D1108608

PAPER C WS

& more Saskatchewan crime stories.

Barb Pacholik
& Jana G. Pruden

2009

The authors may be contacted via the publisher:

CPRC ⟨⨅⟩
P R E S S

Canadian Plains Research Center
University of Regina
Regina, Saskatchewan s4s 0A2
Canada
TEL: (306) 585-4758 FAX: (306) 585-4699
E-MAIL: canadian.plains@uregina.ca
WEB: www.cprc.uregina.ca

Library and Archives Canada Cataloguing in Publication

Pacholik, Barb, 1965-
Paper cows & more Saskatchewan crime stories / Barb Pacholik, Jana G. Pruden.

(TBS, 1482-9886 ; 25)
Includes bibliographical references.
ISBN 978-0-88977-232-8

1. Crime—Saskatchewan—History—20th century. 2. Criminals—
Saskatchewan—History—20th century. I. Pruden, Jana G., 1974– II. University
of Regina. Canadian Plains Research Center III. Title. IV. Series: TBS 25

HV6809.S3P325 2009   364.1'0971240904   C2009-901654-0

Cover and book design: Duncan Campbell
COVER IMAGE: *Portrait of Man Lighting Cigar,* © Veer Incorporated.

Printed and bound in Canada at Friesens.

We acknowledge the financial support of the Government of Canada through
the Book Publishing Industry Development Program (BPDIP) for our publishing activities. We acknowledge the support of the Canada Council for the Arts
for our publishing program.

 Canadian Patrimoine
Heritage canadien
 Canada Council Conseil des Arts
for the Arts du Canada

CONTENTS

Acknowledgments

This book could not have happened without the contributions of many people, for whom we are thankful. To the court staff who unearthed heaps of files—some of which were no small challenge to find or carry—your efforts are appreciated. The fine resources of the National Archives, Saskatchewan Archives, and Regina Public Library Prairie History Room—and the employees who entertained our requests—also played a critical role in our research.

We are thankful to all the journalists who left a paper trail, first covering many of these stories when they made headlines years, decades, and even more than a century ago. Without those efforts, many of these cases would have long been forgotten—or, in the case of Geoffrey Hewelcke, would not have been recorded quite so colourfully. We appreciate the support of our colleagues and management at the *Regina Leader-Post*, and give a special thank you to photographer Bryan Schlosser for his work on the authors' photo.

To those who were a part of these stories, including Gerry Good, Dennis Chisholm, Al Rosseker, Dave Quick, Suzanne Boyer, and many others, thanks for sharing your experiences and fielding questions about the finer details. We also appreciate the tips offered by readers of our first book, *Sour Milk & Other Saskatchewan Crime Stories*. To those who reviewed rafts of drafts, including Ian Hamilton, Evan McIntyre, Mary Scott and one very special person who requested anonymity, we appreciate your thoughts, direction, and pencil marks in the margins.

We are indebted to Brian Mlazgar and the Canadian Plains Research Center for the opportunity to once again bring this alternative social history into being. And last but certainly not least, we thank our friends and families for their unending support and patience as we stole away to immerse ourselves in crime writing.

Authors' Note

When we started work on a follow-up to our true crime collection *Sour Milk,* the question we were most commonly asked was, "Are there enough interesting crimes in Saskatchewan to fill another book?"

After a year of research and writing, our answer is a resounding and unequivocal "yes."

In fact, researching this book turned up tales that, at times, surprised even us. In addition to compelling cases of murder, deceit and fraud, we found frozen gold, herds of paper cows and a mysterious international conspiracy.

We found a suicide bombing, a hijacking and a buxom bootlegger named Tootsie—all right here in the Land of the Living Skies.

In writing these stories, we have recreated the crimes according to what is the most likely course of events based on court documents, transcripts of court proceedings, historical references, newspaper archives, media reports, photographs, and, whenever possible, our own interviews, notes, and observations.

Of course, pinning down the "truth" is a nearly impossible task. The written record of events and people's memories can be spotty and unreliable, and in some cases even confirming a basic bit of information—such as a person's name—can be maddening. There are invariably many different perceptions and recollections of a single event, some of which are vastly divergent from each other. In these situations, we have chosen what we believe to be the most probable "truth" based on all the information before us.

Most of the stories in this book are about a single criminal event, and do not look at the long-term consequences of the crime—or the later actions of the offender. Some of the people in these pages may have made one dreadful or foolish mistake, then gone on to live otherwise laudable lives. Others are incorrigible, destined to life—or death—behind bars.

It should also be said that some of the people in our stories maintained their innocence despite the findings of a judge or jury. In these cases, we have gone with the version of events that satisfied the court—whether that is right or wrong may be up to you to decide.

We have tried not to make any unreasonable inferences or assumptions, and anything that appears in quotes is as it was said, quoted, or recounted by the people involved. When there are grammatical or other errors in a quotation, we have let them stand uncorrected.

Wherever noted, we have used fake names to comply with court-ordered publication bans. These pseudonyms are entirely fictitious, and any resemblance in whole or in part, to real life individuals is entirely coincidental.

Jana G. Pruden and Barb Pacholik
January 2009

"They in whom one has the most implicit confidence can the most easily deceive, if they set out to do so."

—JUSTICE DONALD MACLEAN
REPORT OF THE SASKATCHEWAN CANTEEN FUNDS
INQUIRY COMMISSION, 1940

DEAD PARROTS

The rising sun revealed waves of hard-packed snow, the stubble from last year's crop struggling to poke through. The wind-whipped landscape seemed to go on forever, interrupted only by the odd farm or a scattering of scrubby, skeletal poplars. There is a serene beauty about a winter morning on the Prairies. It would have made a beautiful photograph.

Lights flashed that morning—not from a camera but the strobing red lights on a highway patrol car and the flashlight held in a Mountie's hand. He was using it to peer into the back of a rental van stopped along the Trans-Canada Highway.

Constable Robert Kane had been on his way to set up a speed trap when he noticed the cube van heading east. It seemed to be sitting a bit low, like it was carrying a heavy load. The rental van with Quebec plates pulled to a stop about eight kilometres west of Indian Head in response to Kane's flashing lights.

Leaning out the window, Kane explained to the lone occupant that if the van was hauling a commercial load, the driver required a log book. The 41-year-old driver from Kelowna said he was simply helping out a friend whose father had suffered a heart attack and needed some furniture moved. Kane asked if he could take a look in the back. There had been a lot of contraband—alcohol, drugs, even weapons—moving along this highway, the constable explained.

Operation Pipeline was making a dent in that sort of trafficking. The RCMP program wasn't really so much about pipes, as conduits—a means of carrying illicit goods from one point to the other. The Number One Highway had become Main Street for smugglers. Mounties like Kane were trained to look for the unusual, the things that didn't add up.

"I have no problem with you searching it," the driver told Kane that morning on January 29, 2000 before opening the padlock at the back of the van.

They couldn't get the door open all the way because some of the furniture was jammed against it. Kane squeezed in beside a bookcase, and shone his flashlight on dressers, night tables, cabinets and deacon's benches. They easily filled nearly all of the seventeen-foot-long space. Some of the pieces were askew. The veteran Mountie wondered at the lack of packing blankets to prevent the unfinished furniture from getting damaged.

Now that was unusual.

The driver agreed packing blankets would have made sense, but they had been in a rush. Besides, his friend, who was moving to Montreal, would have no trouble with the repairs. He made a hobby of refinishing furniture, the middle-aged man explained.

Since it appeared the driver lacked the proper documents for hauling a commercial load, Kane started to write out a ticket. But then he had second thoughts, especially when the driver mentioned the furniture refinishing was more hobby than business. Kane decided to give the guy the benefit of the doubt, told him to have a good trip and watched as he drove away.

While Kane had been peering at furniture, Constable David Domoney, who was also supposed to be on the speed trap that morning, was checking out a red 2000 Chev Cavalier. Minutes after Kane stopped the van, the eastbound car suddenly slowed about a kilometre further up the highway and turned right onto a gravel road. A lot of burglaries recently in the area had Domoney wondering why a car with B.C. plates was turning down a back road.

As Domoney pulled his cruiser in behind the rental car, his partner, Auxiliary Constable Hughie Gilchrist, noticed the Cavalier's driver seemed to be looking back towards the highway. Perhaps he had noticed the flashing lights by the cube van. Domoney asked to see the driver's licence. He seemed to be having some trouble locating the rental papers on the car, but finally handed those over too. The driver explained that he'd simply stopped to "take a leak." He was on his way to Montreal to look at some time-share properties in the Laurentians, an ideal spot for a skiing getaway.

While the driver took care of his business near the front of the car, Domoney got into his cruiser to check the name on the licence: Christopher Thomas Speedie of Fanny Bay, B.C. He wasn't wanted, and his licence was valid. Domoney asked if it would be okay to look inside his car.

"Go ahead. There's nothing in there," Speedie replied.

In fact, the Cavalier's trunk held two bags: one black, one white. A small, white garbage bag contained a golf shirt, couple of cheque books, day planner, and cellphone with a laminated business card attached. Speedie explained that they belonged to a friend he had recently met.

Domoney suggested they get out of the cold and climb into the cruiser so he could ask a few more questions.

As Gilchrist looked over the black overnight bag in the trunk, Kane pulled up to see if help was needed. Gilchrist noticed everything in the small carrying case seemed neatly folded. But on top of the clothes sat two running shoes, with socks stuffed inside. It struck Gilchrist as unusual. He pulled the socks from the left runner and saw a thick wad of what appeared to be $100 bills held together by a rubber band. The right runner held a wad of twenties.

Gilchrist showed Kane his find, and Kane, calling Domoney from the cruiser, showed him the money. Speedie quickly offered an explanation. The cash was for his time-share shopping trip. He had another $1,060 bundled up in his right jacket pocket and two cellphones in the left. About that time,

Kane noticed the business card on the cellphone that had been pulled from the white bag.

Kane recognized the name.

It matched the driver of the cube van he had just let go.

The Mounties figured they had seen enough to launch an investigation into proceeds of crime. Constable Ken McLaughlin, off duty, was roused from his home to head down the highway in hopes of intercepting the loaded van. He spotted it near Grenfell, about fifty kilometres from where Kane had watched it leave.

The van was taken to the Broadview RCMP detachment, where Kane got to examine that cargo a little closer. The bookcase blocking the door was moved, as were a few more pieces from the back. The wooden furniture seemed reasonably light, the officers thought. At least, it did until they tried to move a dresser that wouldn't budge. With help, it was moved enough that Kane could open a drawer.

Inside were five perfectly-wrapped, ten-inch-square packages, each about two and half inches thick. Gilchrist let out a whoop. The auxiliary constable, who was a civilian volunteer, had seen things like this in pictures, but never the real stuff.

Kane had his suspicions about what they were, but the unmarked, odourless, brick-like, thirteen-pound packages weren't volunteering information. Gilchrist handed Kane a knife, which he used to slice into a package. There was a hiss as the vacuum seal was broken. Kane tore back the wrapping and stared at black, high-quality hashish.

Realizing they had stumbled upon something big, Kane returned the package to the dresser, sealed up the van and called in the professionals. It took six hours for officers from the drug squad, proceeds of crime unit, and regular members like Kane to find, bag and tag each of the uniform, six-kilogram-bricks of hash. Four packages were strapped inside each one of the thirty deacon's benches. The rest of the bricks were divided among the fourteen remaining pieces of furniture—dressers, washstands, cabinets.

An RCMP officer stands behind 1,200 kilograms of hashish seized by officers after stopping a van on the Trans-Canada Highway on January 29, 2000. Photographer Don Healy, courtesy *Regina Leader-Post.*

Peeling back the outer wrapping revealed vacuum-sealed bags, stamped with a picture of a coffee cup. Inside each "cappuccino pack" were two wafers of plastic-wrapped hash with gold seals that read "Not for sale in the U.S.A." Each brick held a dozen individual packages of hash.

And there were two hundred bricks—a record bust totalling about 1,200 kilograms worth some $7.8 million by the cops' estimate.

Five police cruisers hauled the hash back to an exhibit locker in Regina.

Speedie was also searched that day. His money belt held twenty-eight $100 bills.

Three days before the van was stopped on the highway, it was rented for $2,471, paid in hundreds and twenties, from a business in Duncan, B.C. The clerk remembered the renter quite well because it turned into an all-day transaction. He initially wasn't happy with the van supplied, so switched to a larger one. He didn't like that one either and returned, finally settling for the seventeen-footer. He was moving his girlfriend to Montreal from Vancouver, the renter explained, and she had a lot of antique furniture. The clerk had written down his name, driver's licence and social insurance number. The identification was for Norman Martin Howe, age 51, from Banff, Alberta. Such a picturesque city, renowned for its ski hills.

When she sat in a makeshift courtroom in Broadview, Saskatchewan, seven months later for a preliminary hearing, the clerk had no trouble picking out the man who had rented the van. At that point, he was dressed in blue jeans, a red-flowered shirt and glasses. She pointed to 55-year-old Christopher Speedie.

While the names, ages, and addresses were different, Howe's photograph on his driver's licence and the one on Speedie's passport—seized from his motorhome parked at Vancouver's International Airport—were the same. Speedie was Howe. The real Howe, who had indeed once known Speedie, had died in 1974 at age 25 in a head-on car crash. Somehow, a wallet with identification and active bank cards in his name was in Speedie's motorhome, where police also found $5,700 worth of travellers' cheques, his passport with recent stamps from Holland, Dutch coins and phone cards, and a map of Amsterdam.

Speedie, a well-known freelance photographer, lived off the royalties earned from his photos, mostly of the iconic mountain scenery at Whistler, B.C. His photographs of the so-called Crazy Canucks—the Canadian national ski team in its 1970s and '80s heyday of World Cup victories—appear in books. He had even once photographed Margaret and Pierre Trudeau on their skiing honeymoon at Whistler.

However, Speedie's best-known work is not remembered for its famous faces. He was among a group of hippies who hung out at an abandoned logging camp, known as Toad Hall, near Whistler's slopes in the 1970s. One beautiful, spring morning after a night of partying in 1973, Speedie and thirteen of his ski buddies gathered outside Toad Hall, doffed their clothes, and posed with only their skis, boots and smiles for posterity. Speedie lined everything up before jumping into the front row, first on the left, and having someone else press the shutter on the camera. The legendary "Picture at Toad Hall," as it's known, of the buck-naked ski bums was made into a poster, providing beer money at the time for Speedie and a buddy who helped make it happen. The memorable photo was used nearly two decades later to promote a reunion at the popular ski hill in April 2000.

It surfaced in the *National Post* about the same time its poster boy was in a Saskatchewan courtroom trying to get bail on four drug charges. He was released, once he ponied up $75,000, paid by cheque. Among the three men who acted as sureties on his bail was one of his friends who had also featured prominently in the infamous ski picture.

A Sixties throwback, Speedie was most at home on a ski hill or out fishing with his dog. But his legal woes weren't completely unfamiliar territory. He had been put on trial in 1990 with five other men caught in Operation Trojan Horse. The so-called "reverse sting" by the Mounties and u.s. drug officers had a bogus supplier ship three tonnes of marijuana to the B.C. coast—the first instalment of what police contended was an international conspiracy to import twenty tonnes of high-grade pot from Thailand. (In fact the three tonnes came from previous busts by the u.s. Drug Enforcement Agency.) Two of the smugglers were double agents co-operating with police. As the bales of pot were being unloaded by a crew that included Speedie, undercover cops emerged from below the *Trojan*'s deck and nabbed them easily. The complex trial dragged on for seven months. It made for an intriguing story, and Speedie wrote about the case, including the informants who tattled to the police. He titled his work "Dead Parrots Don't Talk." The cover page had a cartoonish-looking dead parrot with its little feet up in the air.

That case collapsed after two mistrials and more than three years of legal delays. Speedie walked.

But unfortunately for him, the cops in Saskatchewan were good and smart—Sergeant Gerry Good and Constable Frank Smart with the Integrated Proceeds of Crime unit. They and other officers traced the drugs and money all the way to Hungary, where the hash had been packaged, secreted in furniture, and sent to Canada. And they followed the trail to Amsterdam, where the drug-smuggling scheme was cooked up.

Facing four charges, the laid-back ski-bum-photographer-turned-drug shipper began to realize this case wasn't going up in smoke—especially with a new, key witness who had surfaced. Speedie agreed to cut a deal on the hash case. He would plead guilty to two charges and the driver of the van would go free. The deal meant Speedie, then living out of his motorhome and working at a fishing camp on B.C.'s central coast, would be sent to prison for five and a half years. He would also forfeit the $19,785 he had been carrying.

In the end, the government did keep the cash, but not Speedie.

He was due in a Vancouver courtroom on September 26, 2002, to enter his plea and face sentencing. But one day before that could happen, prosecutor Byron Wright got some news he could scarcely believe. In fact, Wright wanted proof and requested fingerprint evidence.

The left thumbprint matched.

Speedie had been found dead on September 25 at Forward Harbour Fishing Lodge.

Despite the odd timing, an autopsy turned up nothing unusual.

Months later, the police informant who was expected to testify about what he knew of the international drug operation was found dead in Holland. The explosion that had killed him made identifying the corpse difficult. His death was deemed a suicide.

RED BLOOD IN THEIR VEINS

I t was the world's greatest melodrama—or at least that's
what the papers were calling it. The show was *The Whip*,
and it came to the Savoy Theatre in Moose Jaw in the fall
of 1918.

"All Men, Women and Children with Red Blood in Their
Veins Will Want to See it," the movie poster promised.

A story in *The Moose Jaw Evening Times* further proclaimed the film's dramatic impact. "It is smart, its people are
well dressed, it has a thrilling intense story ... It tells a love
story and a story of villainy that cannot fail to grip and hold
the attention of every spectator."

* * *

They hadn't been in bed long when Jessie Stephens was awakened by a noise. It sounded like someone was knocking at the
door, and she could hear a woman's voice crying out in the
night.

"Oh let me in, oh let me in," the woman was pleading.
"This man has killed my two babies."

Jessie immediately woke her husband, William, still sleeping soundly beside her. Peering out the bedroom window,
William saw their neighbours, the Bromleys, standing outside
in the dark. Mrs. Bromley was pacing back and forth on the
verandah of her home, wringing her hands frantically.

"Oh, he's killed my two babies, I thought you would have left me them," she cried. "I never thought you would have done it."

"Woman keep quiet," Bromley was saying. "Keep quiet."

William sent Jessie to call the police.

Ben Kyte, who was bringing in his bicycle for the night, also heard the disturbance coming from the Bromley home. He could hear Mrs. Bromley wailing, saying, "Oh my lovely babies, you can't have killed them all."

In the moonlight, Kyte could see that the distraught woman was struggling to get into the house, but her husband was blocking the door to prevent her from entering. When Mrs. Bromley saw Kyte, she cried out to him.

"Oh, Mr. Kyte, I have been downtown for the first time in a month to a picture show, and when I get back he says he has killed my babies," she said.

Kyte turned to Walter Bromley, who looked well-groomed and was neatly dressed in a coat and hat. Bromley seemed eerily calm.

"Did you kill the children?" Kyte asked him.

"Yes," Bromley said quietly. "One of them made me so mad that I killed them all."

Kyte asked if he could go into the house.

"You could, but it will do you no good," Bromley told him. "I would not go if I were you."

The Bromleys were gone by the time police arrived. They simply walked away, heading down Ominica Street East together toward the cemetery, their silhouettes fading into the shadows of the night.

Constable Harry Osmon and Detective Hugh Johnstone arrived to find the house lit, shining like a beacon on the darkened street. The doors to the home were locked, and a crowd was already gathering as a neighbour provided the officers with a key to get inside.

It was the most horrible thing the men had ever seen. There was a tangle of small, pale bodies in the west room of the house, two babies piled on top of a boy on the bed, all three children tangled in the bloody bedclothes. The mattress was soaked with blood, and blood was pooled on the floor nearby. An axe lay on the dresser. There were two older girls in the back room, one on top of the other, both in their nightgowns. Like the other children, the girls were dead, each with a deep, crimson gash across her neck.

The Bromleys turned themselves in at the Moose Jaw police station little more than an hour later, and Walter Bromley immediately confessed to killing all five of his children. He gave the police a razor he'd been carrying in his back pocket. He said he'd used it to slit the children's throats.

* * *

Walter Bromley was born in London, England, but came to Canada in the spring of 1904 to make his living working on a farm. He met Lillian Sugden in Winnipeg, and the two married and had a son, Norman. Four more children followed; the girls, Dulcie and Ivy, were born in quick succession a few years after Norman, and the twins, Doris and Joan, after that.

Walter was well-liked in Winnipeg, regarded by his co-workers at the Dominion Express Company as a cheery fellow with a smile for everyone. "A better-natured man never lived," was how one of his friends described him.

Bromley's boss at Dominion Express, W.J. Shore, said Bromley was a trusted employee with a persistently good humour. No one could make Walter lose his temper, Shore said, even if they tried.

But Bromley had had a difficult upbringing, and traces of it stuck with him all those years later. Some members of his family had been plagued by mental problems, and Bromley himself was an alcoholic. He started drinking when he was 14, and at 35 the bottle was taking its toll, wracking his body with tremors and shakes whenever he was without it.

Bromley's brother-in-law, Geoffrey Smallwood, said the family was very happy, but Walter was by nature docile and cold. The boy, Norman, had problems, too. He was an odd child, disobedient and inattentive, overstrung and nervous. The boy also had an unsettling fondness for sharp things. He liked playing with axes and tools, and sometimes stressed Walter to the end of his patience.

Things got worse when the Dominion Express Company transferred Bromley to Moose Jaw and he was demoted from night foreman to billing clerk. The clerking job meant less pay, and money worries had been starting to weigh on Bromley. The summer of 1918 had been tough all around, the war raging, the flu cutting its ugly path around the world.

On the night of September 17, Lillian put the kids to bed around 8:30 and headed off to the theatre alone to see a show. *The Whip* was on at the Savoy, and it was supposed to be a thrilling and marvelous picture.

Walter had been off work for a few days, and after his wife left for the movie he sat down with a Jesse James book that had been left in the house by the previous residents. He told the police that's what he was doing when he heard the boy cry.

"It was one cry," he said later. "Just a cry."

Walter said he was worried the boy would wake the other children.

"Before I realized what I was doing I grabbed my razor which was in the kitchen and rushed up the stairs and took hold of my boy while he was in the centre bedroom and cut his throat and then covered him up with bedclothes," he told the police.

He said he intended to kill himself, too, but couldn't bear to leave his wife alone with four children to raise, so he killed them all. He lost his nerve before he could turn the razor on himself.

"Just like a dream, you might say," he told the police. "Like an awful dream."

After confessing his crimes, Walter Bromley fell fast asleep in his cell. His wife stayed awake all night. Later, the five children were buried in little white coffins, and Bromley was charged with their murders.

But although the police were glad to have Bromley's confession, some parts of his story didn't make sense. For instance, despite his claims that he had killed the children in a moment of rage, a shirt had been found in the house with blood on the back, and Bromley admitted he'd tied it around himself to protect his clothes at the time of the killings.

"The fact that he tied the shirt around his waist like an apron points strongly to the fact that he meditated upon the deed before he went upstairs," noted one newspaper article.

Some in town believed the act had been prompted by economic hardship. The family's $25 rent was due just two days after the murders, and Mrs. Bromley recalled her husband saying: "I have done away with them all and they will not freeze this winter."

Others believed only insanity could have led Bromley to kill his own children.

In assessing Bromley's mental state, Dr. Robert Burwell took note of Bromley's physical imperfections and considered the family history of insanity, as well as the sheer madness of the crime itself. This was clearly the act of a person not in his right mind, and the doctor concluded Bromley had committed the murders while in "a delirium of the senses."

"He has no hope that I can see," the doctor said.

Precisely what led the good-humoured 35-year-old to slit the throats of his five children didn't much matter to the jury that heard his case inside a packed Moose Jaw courtroom later that fall. After listening to the evidence, the jurors found Walter Bromley guilty of murdering his children, and he was sentenced to hang.

In a letter sent to the minister of justice after the trial, Dr. Gordon Bell described Bromley as a "mental defective of a dangerous type." Since the insane were not hanged, Bell recommended Bromley receive clemency from Ottawa.

"I have no doubt his offence was the product of a disordered brain," Bell wrote.

The minister agreed. The sentence was soon commuted to life in prison, and Bromley began serving his time at the Prince Albert Penitentiary.

Three years later, Lillian Bromley also wrote a letter to the minister of justice.

She said she was glad her husband had not been hanged, and held out some hope that he would one day be freed from prison.

"My husband seems alright now, it seems awful for him to be shut up for life, especially as he is not insane," she wrote.

Lillian Bromley said Walter had been proud and fond of his children, and that the killings could only have taken place in a fit of temporary madness.

"As far as the poor fellow's character goes, there was not a better husband living," she wrote. "I don't ever remember him saying an unkind word to me all the years I was married to him."

She pleaded for a ten-year sentence, and told the minister she would wait for her husband to get out of prison so they could be together once again. Walter Bromley spent twenty years in the Saskatchewan Penitentiary for the murders of his children before being released.

The papers called it the most terrible tragedy in the city's history. An unsurpassed tale of love and villainy—almost like a movie.

CYPRUS

The Boeing 737 had already climbed about ten thousand feet when the man at the front of the plane learned of the man at the back. Flight 71 was barely out of Winnipeg.

Lori Quartz, working in economy class, had noticed Naim Djemal from the moment he joined the flight in Winnipeg on November 29, 1974. He seemed overly nervous and upset, looking all around as if searching for something. Quartz had seen a lot of passengers in her two years working for Canadian Pacific Airlines, but this guy stood out.

Her concern heightened when his trips to the washroom started. He left his aisle seat in the last row and went into the toilet, usually on the starboard side. But he never stayed for more then two or three seconds. He went back and forth several times.

Thinking maybe he was air sick, Quartz asked if Djemal wanted to remove his coat. Djemal declined, then took it off moments later.

Several of the crew members looked at him and smiled, measuring his response. There was none. The look on his face was always the same—dark, nervous, severe.

When Quartz came around with drinks, Djemal chose a rum and cola. Meal service followed, but Djemal in the last row would have to bide his time.

Captain Robert Pitcairn didn't want to look too obvious as he left the cockpit and walked into the cabin in response to

Quartz's concerns. He stopped at three or four seats in the economy section, making small talk with the passengers, before bending down on his knees to speak to a lady with a small child on her lap. They were seated directly across the aisle from Djemal, and Pitcairn used the opportunity to take stock of the passenger. When the captain leaned across the aisle as he stood up, Djemal wouldn't even acknowledge him. Pitcairn leaned in closer, speaking to a woman next to him, asking if she was enjoying the flight. Then the captain quickly stepped into the galley at the rear of the plane, talked with cabin attendant Lena Madsen, who was preparing lunch at the ovens, and once again cast his gaze over at the man in the turtleneck sweater, who simply stared forward.

Djemal's eyes were black and sharp and piercing. He seemed emotionless.

It was a stark contrast to the demonstration of anger, fear and desperation Pitcairn would see when he walked back into the cabin eighteen minutes later.

Djemal was one of the last passengers to get his meal tray. Yet, even then he didn't dig into his food, but rather moved it aside to walk to the washroom once more. He opened first one door and peered inside, then the other. When purser Gayle Fortt asked if he was ill, he ignored her.

Fortt was midway up the cabin when she heard the scream from the galley.

Lena had been there alone making coffee when Djemal walked in with a knife in his hand. He jumped behind Lena before she realized what was happening and began stabbing her at the side of her neck. She screamed, hoping it would bring help.

Quartz tried to assist. She grabbed Djemal's shoulders, yelling at him to stop hurting Lena. Only when he turned around did she notice the knife in his hand. She backed off, staring helplessly as Djemal continued stabbing Lena's head as she lay on the floor. The 21-year-old attendant tried to block the blows, which served to fuel Djemal's anger. Quartz stood in the aisle, shouting at him to stop.

"Cyprus," Djemal kept repeating. "Go to Cyprus." In between his shouts, he jabbed at Lena's cheek, forehead, and neck. He threatened to poke her in the eye if she didn't keep her hands down. When he wasn't stabbing her, he kept the knife to her throat. His friends had been killed in Cyprus; he needed to get there.

"Cyprus! Cyprus!" the 30-year-old yelled.

Quartz tried to tell him it wasn't Lena's fault and not to hurt her. "It wasn't anybody's fault," she said. Djemal didn't seem to hear.

"They killed my friends," he kept repeating.

Fortt saw Lena covered in blood, the knife in Djemal's hand, and she ran towards the front of the plane. Then on her return from the cockpit, Fortt urged Djemal to pick up the phone in the galley and speak directly to the captain. Djemal declined.

"Take this plane to Cyprus and go fuck yourself," he replied.

Captain Pitcairn returned to the cabin.

Keeping his voice level and calm, the 36-year-old pilot explained to Djemal that the plane was small and couldn't make it to Cyprus without refuelling. It took some talking, but Pitcairn finally convinced the hijacker to agree to a stop in Saskatoon for fuel. Before walking back to the cockpit, Pitcairn asked Djemal not to hurt Lena anymore.

The attendant, on the job with CP Air for barely eight months, lay on the floor. The captain's words did not stop the assault. Djemal delivered a few more blows, sending blood running into her eyes and ears. He complained it was getting on his pants.

Djemal heard the captain's voice over the public address system, telling the eighty passengers they were making an unplanned stop in Saskatoon because a man had taken over the plane. Djemal grabbed a tighter hold of the bun on the top of Lena's head, kept his knee on her chest, and held the knife to her throat—his way of preparing for landing.

As the plane descended through the clouds, the ground getting closer, it was as if something dark in Djemal lifted and reason returned.

"Do you want the knife?" he asked Lena. But she was too frightened and in shock to realize what he was asking. "Please don't hurt me anymore," she pleaded.

Quartz walked over to the galley upon their arrival. "What do you want us to do?"

"Get the police," came Djemal's startling reply.

Pitcairn told his co-pilot to make a quick exit if things went wrong—one fewer pilot to fly this plane to Cyprus, the better, he thought. He instructed Quartz to assist at least some of the passengers in leaving the plane. Then he walked back to the galley.

"What can we do for you now?" Pitcairn asked.

Djemal stood and approached the captain. "I surrender to you. Take me to the police. I don't care now. I want to surrender." He handed Pitcairn the knife.

Only then did the captain notice the initials on the silver handle: "CP Air." It was a knife from the dinner tray.

The captain retrieved Djemal's bag from the cabin and walked up the aisle to exit. Djemal was thirsty. So the man in control of the plane and the one who had assumed that role for about half an hour stopped at first class and each had a drink of water. Djemal was frightened his baggage would be lost once he was arrested. Pitcairn reassured him, walking outside the plane to the luggage compartment to show Djemal he couldn't open the locked hatch, but promising to find someone who could. Djemal gave the captain his ticket and baggage tags as Pitcairn escorted him to the officers waiting on the tarmac.

Two hours later, Pitcairn was back in the cockpit. After the plane was combed for bombs, Flight 71 resumed its trip to Edmonton, then Vancouver.

This time, Lena Madsen, from North Burnaby, B.C., was among the passengers. She had received stitches for the gashes in her forehead and each cheek. The remaining cuts fortunately were superficial.

Back in the 1970s—when CP Airlines still took to the skies, captains visited with passengers, hot meals were served on domestic flights, and airline cutlery wasn't plastic—hijacking was a new offence. It had been on the books only two years. And now Djemal would become one of the first Canadian cases.

Originally from Cyprus, the naturalized Canadian citizen was stunned by news of his friends' deaths during the fighting back in his homeland. He stopped sleeping and eating. He was taking sleeping pills, but they didn't help. He could only envision the terrible deaths his friends had suffered. As his depression deepened, he became focused, maybe even obsessed, on getting his family to Turkey from Cyprus by whatever means necessary.

Six days before Flight 71, he was taken off a plane in Calgary and transported to hospital by ambulance when he became ill. He was prescribed more sleeping pills and a vitamin supplement.

Two psychiatrists suggested the hijacking, driven by Djemal's depression, was out of character. His lawyer urged the judge to have compassion and consider how this began, and how it ended.

"Truth is stranger than fiction," Cal Tallis told the court.

The case was heard by Judge Robert H. King, who two years earlier had found a Saskatoon theatre guilty of showing obscene entertainment, a movie called *The Stewardesses*. And now he found the terror inflicted on a young, innocent stewardess and a plane full of passengers was also offensive.

King focused on stopping things before they started, by imposing a sentence he hoped would deter others who might commit such brazen acts. The judge sentenced Djemal to seven years in prison.

It was the same day Turkey pulled out of peace talks with Cyprus.

A FAITHFUL WIFE

Johnnie woke up around eight that morning, roused by the daylight streaming into the small farmhouse and the sounds of the kids. The 9-year-old had been sleeping in the kitchen, and when he opened his eyes he saw his little brother and sister, Harry and Lena, playing in the main room of the farmhouse just a few feet away. Their mother usually slept in the room, too, but she wasn't in there with them that morning. Maybe up and working already. Harry and Lena crawled into bed with Johnnie for a few minutes, and they all played and giggled together. Then Harry got up and padded into their dad's small bedroom.

"Johnnie come here," the 6-year-old called a moment later.

"Father is dead," he said. "See how much blood there is?"

Walking into the bedroom, Johnnie saw. He saw their father lying still and ashen on the bed with his hands folded on his chest, the sheet pulled over crossed legs. There was a gaping hole near their father's ear, and another hole in the pillow beneath his head. There was a trickle of blood, and part of their father's head was gone. Feathers from the punctured pillow drifted and swirled around the room.

Johnnie picked up the gun lying on the bed and cracked it open. There were two shells inside, one of which was spent.

Then the neighbour, John Kokunuk, came knocking at the door, looking to pick up some wheat.

"Father is dead," Johnnie told him, pulling the door open so Kokunuk could come inside.

* * *

Alec and Grapena Shulman had been married for eleven years, and there hadn't been many good times between them. They fought a lot from the beginning, arguing about money and everything else there was to fight about.

"I was beaten up and chased everywhere," Grapena said once. "Practically all my married time, right from the beginning since I got married."

He beat her with his hands, with a leather strap, with a horse whip. The first time had been a few months after they got married, and it was every week after that. Sometimes every day.

She got away from Alec once and went to stay with her father, but he sent her back home. "You married him," her father had told her.

Another time Grapena fled all the way to Manitoba. She found work in Roblin, had a place to live and was doing fine there, but Alec found her and took her back to the farm. Grapena even went to a lawyer once, but the lawyer again sent her back to him, resolving the situation by telling Alec not to abuse his wife anymore.

Alec got charged after one of the beatings and had to go to court, where the judge made him pay $100 for his crime.

Grapena wasn't the only one to feel the force of Alec's hand. One day he beat Johnnie with a horse strap, pummeling the boy until Grapena got between them and took the blows instead. Once Alec punched and beat her in front of the children because she didn't have time to sew some buttons for him.

Teddy Babiuk stayed with the Shulmans in May of 1918 and saw one of their fights for himself. He remembered Alec telling Grapena she was a devil, and that God would help him get rid of her.

"Did you hear what Alec said?" Grapena asked Teddy later, as she milked a cow in the barn and he tended to the horses.

"I certainly did," Teddy told her.

"The devil will take him out of here before he will take me," she vowed. "He will have to go first."

It was not the only time she made such a vow.

"If he beat me up once more I will shoot him or I will stab him," Grapena told her friend Rosie that summer. "I will cut him with a knife."

Increasingly, Grapena had been confiding in Frank Rutka, a man Alec had hired as a farmhand. Rutka lived out in the granary, and he and Grapena had slowly become close. Frank certainly had no love for his boss. He didn't like how Alec treated Grapena, but Frank had his own problems with the man, too. He had once discovered his own wife lying with Alec in a field.

Grapena knew about the women. Alec was with lots of women during their marriage. He even brought one to live with them once, sometime in 1914 or 1915, and the woman stayed with them for two years, sleeping with Alec as his wife, while Grapena slept with the children in another room.

She found the rifle in July. It was hidden in the granary and wrapped in a horse blanket, and Grapena thought Alec was probably going to shoot her with it. At first she was going to take the gun to the police, but instead she showed it to Frank and he taught her how to load it, helping her to aim it, showing her where to put her hands when she pulled the trigger. Grapena hid the rifle in the floorboards under the house, in case she wanted—or needed—to use it.

* * *

Alec came home late on the night of September 28, 1918. He had been over at John Kokunuk's that evening, working out the details of a steer deal they were planning. He had been in a fine mood over there, laughing and talking with Kokunuk for hours, but his mood changed when he walked into the house.

Grapena was ill. She'd been pregnant, but lost the baby three days earlier from the worry and the beatings. She was standing in the kitchen when he walked in, and there was something about it that made him angry. That time, he used a stick, beating his wife with it until he tired, then going off to bed.

After the beating, Grapena went to talk to Frank, then she got the gun. She was wearing only a nightshirt and slippers when she crept to the side of her husband's bed, raised the rifle, and shot him in the head while he slept.

"Up until the last moment I was beaten," she would say later, remembering that night.

After listening to the case over two days at the Yorkton courthouse in January of 1919, twelve men took less than an hour to find Grapena Shulman guilty of murdering her husband. It was the first time in the province's history that a woman had been convicted of murder.

"She received her sentence stoically, the foreman of the jury exhibiting more signs of emotion than she did," a newspaper reporter in the courtroom observed.

Recognizing Grapena's difficult life and the brutal treatment she endured at the hands of her husband, the jury made a strong recommendation for mercy. But the noose knows no mercy, and a death sentence was the only penalty for murder at the time. Grapena Shulman was to be hanged on April 22. Court of King's Bench Justice Hector MacDonald told her he would inform officials in Ottawa about the case, but held out little hope for a lesser penalty.

"You had better prepare yourself for the end in the meanwhile," he advised.

The jury was shocked. They had never intended the woman to die. Almost immediately, the twelve men penned a petition demanding that her life be spared.

"Had we known that the judge had not the power to reduce the penalty from death sentence to a term in prison, we certainly would not have brought the accused in guilty of murder," they wrote.

The jurors said Grapena Shulman had a terrible life, and had been brutally wronged and treated inhumanely by her husband. They saw her as a good woman, a loving mother and a faithful wife who had maintained a sweet disposition despite her terrible circumstances. They said Grapena was under immense mental and physical strain before she killed Alec, and was dominated by the hired man, Frank Rutka. The jurors not only opposed the death penalty, they recommended that Grapena serve the shortest sentence possible for killing her husband—preferably a term of less than two years.

The twelve men took the petition back to their home communities and beyond, quickly gathering thousands of signatures in support of saving the woman they had condemned to die. Their pleas were persuasive.

Two weeks before Grapena Shulman was to hang, the mother of four had her sentence commuted to life in prison. She was sent to the Kingston Penitentiary, where she would be housed in a segregated unit for women.

In the spring of 1923, Shulman wrote a letter to the government pleading for her release.

"I am asking this favour for my Dear children's sake," she wrote. "I will be so greatful to you if you will release me so I can go home to my loved ones, and I truly promise I will never give you any cause to regret my release."

She was let out of prison a year later, having served five years for the murder of her husband. She went back to the farm to live a quiet life with her children.

PAPER COWS

City slickers from the bank showed up every three months or so.

In Brian's opinion, they had no idea what a cow looked like, let alone how to count the stock or check for brands.

The bean-counters from the big city casually surveyed the corral where the cattle roamed. "Well, how many do you think there are in there, Brian?"

Brian Oviatt would take a gander and come up with the right answer. "I don't know—fifty, or one hundred, or sixty"— whatever number might be needed in the circumstances. And whatever Brian said, that's what the auditor wrote down. Sometimes when Brian wasn't available, his father-in-law Roy Traynor helped tally up the cattle. After all, the livestock were being fattened up at his feedlot, the Diamond-T Cattle Company.

The Saskatoon bank would often call on a Monday to say someone would be out in a few days to count the cattle. Brian, in turn, called Roy, who would suggest holding the bank off for a bit until he could get a few more cattle moving around in the pen. At times, he moved in calves from another ranch and had them mingle with those held by Diamond-T. If you didn't know exactly what you were looking for, it would be simple to mistake all two hundred head as belonging to the same herd.

But if you looked closely, you would probably discover only about twenty-five actually had the appropriate brand.

It was that easy.

* * *

Leroy Traynor, Roy to most people, had built a sizeable grain and cattle farm that stretched from Delisle to Donavon. The father of eight considered it a family operation. Four of the boys were directly involved, with the head of the family steering them in the right direction. Roy was also a leader in his community, active in the local 4-H Club, a committee chair for the Saskatoon Exhibition, and a cattle show judge at Canadian Western Agribition in Regina. Some thought of Roy as Saskatchewan's own Ben Cartwright: an astute cattleman, respected, respectable, and downright charismatic.

The farm expanded in the 1980s—then interest rates sky-rocketed, land values fell, and grain prices plummeted. The banks foreclosed, and moved to repossess Traynor's land. His son-in-law Brian, who saw in Roy a father figure, led the fight at the farmgate, rallying together family, friends, and neighbours to keep the bankers away. They tried, anyway. The bank still took the land, but Roy had the right to match the highest bid and buy it back when the land went up for sale. It was akin to waving a Grade A steak in the face of a penniless man. Sure he could have it—but only if he could find the money.

A miner by trade, Brian set up a cattle co-operative in late 1986 at Roy's urging. The program had been developed by the provincial government to give a kick to the ailing agriculture industry by helping people invest in cattle with borrowed money. Co-op members bought cattle in the co-operative, the banks loaned them the money, and the government guaranteed part of the loan. When the cattle were sold, the loan was paid and any profit pocketed.

Brian Howard Oviatt became the supervisor of the Flat-lands Cattle Co-op, securing loans, buying and selling cattle, and updating the bank. It grew to a hundred members.

That's how it all worked on paper.

In reality, Flatlands became Roy Traynor's cash cow.

Most cattle purchased by the co-operative went to Traynor's Diamond-T feedlot near Delisle, generating business for him.

But many of Flatlands' cattle actually roamed only through Roy and Brian's imaginations. They existed on signed agreements, invoices, audits, and tax returns. Brian skilfully worked those paper cows, like a master of origami.

In the co-op's early years, Roy recruited investors, who agreed to the use of their names to help him out. Sometimes Roy even paid the $1,250 fee required by the bank to open the line of credit. Two board members had to sign every purchaser agreement, but eventually they pre-signed a stack of forms to fast-track the paperwork, with the blessing of the government. The agreements went to the bank, and the bank issued loans to Flatlands, ostensibly to buy cattle for the investors.

Loans had to be paid off within a year. Sometimes Flatlands sold the cattle and used the proceeds to pay off the loan. Flatlands would then buy them back (at a slightly higher rate because of the cattle dealer's commission), using another loan. There was even a name for it—cattle flipping. It was all done on paper. The cattle never left the lot.

The bulk of the cash generated by the scheme went to Roy Traynor. Initially, it gave Roy, who couldn't get any credit because of his bankruptcy woes, some much-needed moolah to operate his cattle ranch.

Once his land went on the market, Flatlands was the means to an end. He had out-smarted the bankers at their own game, using the money they thought they were loaning to cattle investors to buy back his land that the banks had repossessed.

It looked like the jig was up in 1989 when a nosy auditor began asking questions. And some of the investors didn't have answers. They didn't seem to know anything about the cattle purchased in their names. Roy smoothed things over with them, and the auditor chalked it up to a misunderstanding.

Flatlands kept on going, securing more loans to pay off the outstanding ones. Between 1989 and 1991, signatures were forged on eighty purchaser agreements. Brian admitted using a light table to trace signatures onto about fifteen. It remains a mystery who did the rest. But clearly Brian kept the books in this fiction.

The beginning of the end came in September 1991 when Flatlands needed a lot of cash to pay off loans. Brian sent over nine forged documents for the purchase of $400,000 worth of cattle. The bank still put out the loans, but staff were suspicious about some of the signatures. The bank eventually uncovered the forgeries, and an audit revealed a shortage of about 1,300 head of cattle, most of which had never actually existed. A two-year RCMP investigation followed.

By then Brian had also reached his own personal breaking point. Towards the end, other farmers were phoning him to say they didn't have enough money to put in crops, and they too wanted to buy some paper cows. He wound up hospitalized for eight months with a mental breakdown.

"I turned myself into somebody that I could cope with, somebody that could lie and cheat every day of the week. When I looked in the mirror, I didn't like who I was looking at."

Roy paid Brian a visit at his hospital bedside and offered to buy his silence. Brian turned him down.

By the time the dust on the paper trail settled, the bank had loaned about $2.2 million based on forged documents, although half had been repaid to satisfy loans. The Mounties estimated the paper cow caper had wrangled about $785,000 cash from the bank. Taxpayers were also partially on the hook since the loans were secured by the provincial government.

A total of $623,000 was traced back to Diamond-T. Almost half was used to keep the company operating. Roy used $350,000 to buy thirteen quarter-sections of land, which went back to the bank when the scheme fell apart. His lawyer, Si Halyk, said Roy saw an opportunity to "borrow" money, believing he would repay it with income generated by the farm.

Brian Oviatt's bank accounts reaped about $85,000, although his lawyer said his client actually pocketed only $17,000. The rest went to Diamond-T to pay fictitious feed bills for non-existent cattle.

"There is a real connection between a farmer and his dirt," Brian's lawyer, Bill Wardell, explained to the court at the sentencing for fraud in 1994. Brian would do anything to help his desperate father-in-law, who once threatened to shoot himself if he lost any of his land.

When Brian took the witness stand against Roy, he could not look him in the eye. Asked why, he replied, "I love him."

Roy Traynor, a first-time offender at age 65, was sentenced to twenty-two months in jail for fraud.

As the prosecution saw it, Roy had roped Brian into the misdeeds. "What we have here is an individual who is somewhat like a hired arsonist," Crown prosecutor Terry Hinz said.

The judge sentenced Brian to three years of probation and six months of electronic monitoring in his own home. The 42-year-old, who also suffered bankruptcy and a failed marriage, was ordered to pay back $17,000.

"It was all so simple to do at the time," he told the court.

"We were handed things on a platter by the bank, by the government: people signing blank feeder agreements; board members being asked to sign blank feeder agreements in advance—a book of them in advance; the bank saying that you could flip people over just on paper, just so it looked good at the bank. It was just too easy. And nobody realized what was going on."

Like cows to the slaughter.

TOOTSIE'S OATH

Christmas garlands strung around the room and greeting cards on the table fixed the month at December. On the blood-spattered calendar with the portrait of Jesus, time stood still at 1953.

The same couldn't be said of the mostly mummified body entombed in this room, discovered when a skeleton key forced open the lock. The months and seasons had taken their toll on the body of Mihaill John Todor, Mike or John as his friends called him. They knew him for his neat grey mustache, prominent nose, and thick eyebrows.

But the police officers who found John could not easily forget what he had become. At funerals, death looks sterile, clean and peaceful. John was none of these things. Maggots and flies littered the bed where his corpse hung over the edge. Decomposition had long since caved in his breast bone. Even the pillow, once beneath his head, had rotted. The long fleece underwear covering the cadaver neck to ankle was still discernable, but John's right sock had disappeared. His false teeth, still waiting for him to awaken, lay on the bedside table next to a Romanian psalm book; pencil marks denoted John's favourites. A thick film of dust blanketed everything in the room.

Even more overwhelming than the sight was the smell, which would linger in memories long after it left the nostrils. The foul odour of neglected death permeated the air—despite the Airwick air freshener someone had placed futilely beneath one of the windows.

It wasn't the only attempt to mask the death. Pages of the *Saskatchewan Farmer* newspaper, dated June 9, 1954, were pasted on the windows beneath closed blinds. Rags had been packed around the door frame, blue-coloured tissue paper stuffed in the keyhole.

On the other side of that door was the kitchen, littered with discarded tin cans, cartons of empty beer bottles, and decaying food. Next to the cupboards were two pails: one containing slop water, the other rotten sauerkraut. Like the air freshener, some attempt at improvement had been made, evidenced by the empty can of Ridsect fly killer. Bodies of dead flies swept up with dirt from the floor had been tossed in the fire box of the wood stove. In amongst them was a partially burned letter addressed to Todor.

Sixteen months had passed since friends had seen John. His daughter Mary couldn't understand why her letters had gone unanswered. Her inquiries brought a lawyer and two detectives to the three-room bungalow in the spring of 1955. Breaking the padlock on the outer door at 1849 McKay Street, and another on the centre room kitchen, they eventually got to John, or at least what remained of him.

At 74 years of age, any number of things might have taken his life. But a pathologist felt certain a hammer was the most likely explanation. John's skull had been crushed with considerable force, spattering blood on the ceiling and walls.

In his left hand, he still grasped eighty-one hairs, seventy brown and eleven white, that had been pulled out by the roots.

* * *

Carol Fisher last saw her friend and neighbour two days before Christmas in 1953 when she went to his house to get her decorations and tree stand. Born in Romania, John celebrated Orthodox Christmas a week later, so each year when Fisher no longer had any use for her tree, her frugal friend would re-use it for his own celebration. John invited Carol to join him for his Christmas dinner. He planned to roast a duck.

She arrived at the little stucco bungalow around noon on January 7, 1954, and was greeted not by John, but by Elizabeth LeFleche and her roommate Ted Walters. The door to the front room, where John slept, was closed.

LaFleche, or "Tootsie" as she was commonly known, had moved in with John about a month earlier. She had started out as his housekeeper. Widowed in the 1930s, John had confided in Fisher that Tootsie—his junior by four decades—was his woman.

Tootsie told Fisher that John was out of town.

Fisher and other friends came back several more times looking for John. He was in Dysart or Kayville or Windsor or Cupar, Tootsie told them. The locations varied, but the message was the same: John was away, and Tootsie was in charge. Often on the weekends, she was there with another man, Jacob A. Dyck.

Fisher became concerned when the months passed without any sign of her friend. She pressed police to make inquiries. They were told he had gone to Windsor to visit his son. The matter was left in the hands of Todor's lawyers.

By the summer of 1954, the door to 1849 McKay Street had been padlocked and the house abandoned, or so it seemed. As it was on their list of vacant houses, Regina police officers routinely walked around outside the house. No one went inside until April 15, 1955.

* * *

With the discovery that John had never left home, police had a few questions for the people who had lived with his corpse.

Ted Walters had moved in about a week after New Year's and left in the summer. He noticed a smell and the flies but couldn't put his finger on exactly what it was. "I never knew," the 61-year-old would later swear in court.

Jacob Dyck and Tootsie LaFleche, 1955. Reproduced with permission from the *Regina Leader-Post*.

Joseph Jakubco had rented the rear bedroom of John's home for about three years. He heard loud talking and dancing in the kitchen the last night he saw John. The next day, Tootsie told him John had gone to visit his son. Jakubco, too, dismissed the stench.

Tootsie and Jacob Dyck had moved away to work on a farm. Dyck was out milking cows when Tootsie heard the radio reports that they were wanted for questioning by the police. Dyck would later say it was his idea to turn themselves in. He telephoned from the town of Liberty to say they were on their way, and they walked into the Regina police station not long after.

Neither would see liberty again for some time.

In the next year, through an inquest, preliminary hearing, and four trials, Tootsie LaFleche would be called a lot of things. She was a bootlegger—but then so was John—and a woman of loose morals. First married at age 13, she had been divorced a few times and married to at least five husbands. The last one was John Todor, although she had at least two lovers during the marriage, the most current being "Jake" Dyck. Tootsie was an alcoholic and a drug addict who had spent time in an institution taking "the cure." A psychiatrist once said the 36-year-old had the mind of a child one-third her age, yet Dyck's defence lawyer would call her cunning, shrewd, and diabolical. The description most often used with her name was unmitigated liar.

She was also the prosecution's star witness against Dyck.

"She is a creature of a lower order who is practically always in heat and to a considerable extent her evidence is not reliable. However, she is one of the actors in this piece and we do not have the chance to pick or choose our witnesses," Crown prosecutor Robert Barr told one of the three juries to hear Tootsie testify.

A tough-looking, 215-pounder with a no-nonsense stare and sharp tongue to match, Tootsie drew spectators like flies to honey. More than a hundred people packed the courtroom while another fifty lined the hallway waiting for a seat to watch.

She didn't disappoint.

Asked about becoming "friendly" with Jake, Tootsie fired back, "Am I on a charge of morals here?"

Grilled by Jake's lawyer, W. Lloyd Hipperson, about once hitting a man over the head with a lantern, Tootsie denied ever actually striking him.

"I swung the lantern, though."

At each of her lover's three murder trials, Tootsie told her story. On December 31, 1953, Jake had just walked out of prison after serving thirty days for theft. The 45-year-old labourer and Tootsie were accused of stealing some furniture from another of her former paramours. Jake would insist the theft was all Tootsie's doing, but he went to jail for it. She didn't.

Tootsie became restless on New Year's Eve after having a bit too much of John's homemade wine. (She liked to add sugar to give it more zip.) Around midnight, she decided to take a walk. John didn't want her to go, but Tootsie was her own woman.

During her outing, she ran into Jake, and they went back to Todor's house. Tootsie knocked on the window and, dressed only in his long underwear, Todor let them inside. As Tootsie told it, after a few drinks she became even more "plastered," while Jake and John got into an argument. Jake accused the old man—rumoured to have money sewn into his mattress—of not paying him enough for a painting job. According to Tootsie, Jake followed John into the front room, then she thought she heard the elderly man crying, "Why? Why? Why?"

Another witness told the court the Romanian word "vai," which sounds a lot like "why," means "it hurts."

Tootsie said she went into the room to find John dead, and Jake with a hammer in his hand. She kept $200 from Todor's wallet, and, Tootsie swore, she later saw Jake with $1,500 of John's money. Apparently, Jake then buried the cash in a field but lost it when horses knocked down the marker.

A week after John's death, Tootsie was downstairs getting coal when a drop of blood fell on her hand through a crack in the ceiling. She decided to paper up the windows in his room to keep it cooler. Later, she sprayed for flies, put in the air freshener, and sealed the crack around the door.

Jake suggested Tootsie's testimony reeked as badly as Todor's house.

The short, burly man had a wooden left leg, the real one having been amputated near the hip. He told the jury there was no way he could have covered the distance Tootsie claimed and been back at his friend's place, where he celebrated the birth of a new year, not the death of an old man.

As far as he knew, the packing around John's door was to keep out a draft and the smell came from the root cellar, where meat and vegetables were rotting. At Tootsie's request, he bought some fly killer and air fresheners.

The defence painted Tootsie as a filthy liar. She did bring on some of the name-calling herself. In her first statement to police, she had falsely accused another man and woman of Todor's murder. Then in the midst of Dyck's second trial, she admitted having taken her own secret oath in earlier proceedings against him.

"I swore to tell the truth, the whole truth and anything but the truth because I knew I was going to lie," she told a stunned courtroom.

The prosecutor conceded it would be too dangerous to convict on Tootsie's evidence alone. But Barr asked jurors to convict the accused by a hair, which he argued supported Tootsie's version of events.

The eighty-one hairs stuck in the corpse's hand were compared to Tootsie, John himself, and five other people who had frequented the house. The only hair with similar features belonged to Jake Dyck, who suggested they were planted there.

After two hung juries, it was the prisoner's turn to hang. Convicted of murder, Jake's date with the gallows was set for July 24, 1956.

As Dyck's trial ended, Tootsie's began, and this time she never stepped into the witness box. She was convicted of being an accessory to murder for helping her boyfriend avoid detection. The first-time offender was sentenced to five years in prison.

Meanwhile, Dyck appealed his murder conviction. Not surprisingly, the appellate judges dismissed Tootsie as a perjurer and found the hair evidence thin. Ten days before he was to hang, the appeal court overturned his conviction. The Crown opted not to proceed with a then-unprecedented fourth trial.

While in cells at the Regina police station after her arrest, Tootsie had penned a one-page letter addressed "Dear Mother." Born in France, Tootsie moved to Scotland as a youngster, and it was there her mother was murdered. Foster parents took her to Edmonton when she was 6. Seven years later, she was on her own. Her letter was found torn to shreds:

"By this time you've read the papers and no doubt think I'm guilty. I'm not. I never did this horrible, terrible thing I'm accused of.

"I vowed a long time ago that I'd never ask for your help and I'm not asking, not yours or anyone else's. I'm sorry for everything and I realize too that I'm just as guilty as the one that did do it.

"For me, my life is over. Every day the burden is a little harder to bear."

Tootsie served her sentence for being an accessory to murder—a crime no one was ever convicted of committing—at Kingston's Prison for Women. Shortly after her release, Tootsie was found dead at the side of an Ontario highway, the victim of a traffic accident.

SOLDIER OF MISSED FORTUNE

The passenger train had just left the station at Condie when Paul Venzke heard a knock on the end door of the express car. Expecting one of his co-workers, Venzke lifted the iron bar and slid open the door. He didn't recognize the face staring back at him. It was half-covered by a black handkerchief, revealing only a man's blue eyes. However, Venzke's focus wasn't so much on the face as on the hand. It held a revolver.

"Hands up," came the voice behind the handkerchief.

Venzke had his own revolver in a holster at his side. The robber, stepping inside the car, quickly relieved the trainman of that baggage. He picked rope off the floor, bound his prisoner to a steam pipe, gagged him with two handkerchiefs, and helped himself to the keys in Venzke's pocket. They opened the strong box, where the masked man found what he sought.

The robber knew the express car carried cash collected up and down the line by the Canadian National Railway. The masked man tore open a few of the bundles, packed up the rest, and prepared for his journey.

He knew to stay in the express car until the train slowed and changed engines at North Regina. That's when he jumped free, as the train was starting to move again. He carried his loot by the Waterloo Threshing Machine Company on South Railway Avenue and took cover from the cold under a platform at the rear of the building near the CNR tracks. He ripped open the parcels and pocketed a little more than $1,300.

By the time Venzke managed to wriggle free seconds later and pull the emergency air line to halt the train, the bandit was gone.

Police found only the train robber's tracks in the snow.

"He must have been a railroad man to know just how to do it and when to do it," one of the CNR workers told the local newspaper that evening. The "when" was February 1, 1923— the day the express carried the monthly remittances.

The police manhunt continued into the night as a bitter blizzard raged. The rookie train robber was already hunkered down, having taken a room at the Great War Veterans Building.

The masked man's description was on the radio within hours of the brazen robbery. At the request of the police, CKCK, launched only seven months earlier, broke its silence that Thursday night to seek the public's help in finding the stocky, five-foot-eight suspect in the green-checked mackinaw, dark cap and felt boots. The plea was to no avail.

The robber seemed to have made a clean getaway—until police found their lead in the laundry.

A khaki silk handkerchief that had been used to gag Venzke still bore a bit of white tape with the initials D.L., a laundry mark. Police scoured laundries in the city, looking for anyone who recognized it. Finally at Regina Steam Laundry a worker identified the mark as that of Douglas L. Curtis, who had brought in his last load almost three weeks earlier. His clean clothes had been dropped off at a boarding house, but Curtis had left there some time back.

Police learned Curtis had moved to the city in September 1922 and taken a job as a spare brakeman for the CNR. It was the same month an employee named William Lamont Purvis, a conductor, had been fired by the CNR in Edmonton for "unbecoming conduct and false statements in connection with the delay of trains."

Leon Van Gorder was watching the trains come and go at Union Station two days after the robbery when a man rushing towards CNR Train Number Five caught his eye. The 30-year-old man, dressed in a blue suit and carrying a black valise, had a ticket to Saskatoon. He was anxious not to miss his ride.

The would-be passenger grew more confident with each step towards the train. Van Gorder's confidence was also increasing as he approached his target.

"Hey Purvis," Detective-Sergeant Van Gorder of the Saskatchewan Provincial Police shouted. He suspected the fleeing man was William Lamont Purvis, also known as Douglas or Doc Curtis and Douglas Lamont Purvis.

"You have the wrong man," the traveller replied.

But there was no doubt Van Gorder had the right one when he opened the man's valise and found $1,294.50 packed inside—nearly all of the stolen cash. Most of it was stuffed in felt boots in the bag. Purvis's sleeve protectors carried a few 25¢ bills, the ones called "shinplasters." His revolver, an Iver Johnson .32-calibre, was also in his valise. The money that was missing had been used to buy a few meals, the new shirt he was wearing, and the train ticket he had hoped would help him return to his family in Vermilion, Alberta.

At that point, Purvis, for that was his real name, realized he had few options but to co-operate. He took the officer back to the Veterans, where they found the mackinaw and cap worn in the robbery stuffed up in the rafters. In the coat pocket was a black handkerchief, the one that had masked his face.

Purvis also took him down to the warehouse near the tracks, where lay the discarded parcels and paper. Among them was $40—money Purvis had missed in his haste.

Their last stop was the police station, where Purvis wrote out a confession. He explained how he had worked for the CPR in Ontario for a couple of years as a brakeman before taking a similar job with the CNR in Edmonton. He had enlisted with the Canadian Overseas Expeditionary Force in that city on January 5, 1915. Back then he used his real name, Douglas

Lamont Purvis. He went to France with the 49th Battalion, and suffered gunshot wounds on three occasions: to his right shoulder, his head and right hand in another incident, and to both his legs. Discharged honourably in 1919, Corporal Purvis received three medals, including the Victory. However, the former soldier would actually feel far more defeated than victorious in the years after his return to Canada.

Purvis went back to work for the CNR. When the railway company fired him in Edmonton, he reinvented himself in Regina as D.L. Curtis and got on as a brakeman—until the CNR put a stop to that job at the start of December. He had only twenty-five cents in his pocket when he went looking for work on January 31. The next day, he had a small fortune.

"I am a married man and have a wife and year-old baby to support. At that time they had only $20 on which to live. I also owed two months' rent and electric light bill," his confession read.

"The fact that I was so hard up and had to do something for my wife and child was what made me think of holding up the CNR Express Messenger.

"I have never been under arrest before and this is the first offence I have ever committed. I realize the seriousness of this offence and if given a chance, will never violate the laws again," he concluded the five-page statement, signing W.L. Purvis with a flourish. He pleaded guilty three days later, throwing himself on the mercy of the court.

"I have for years been the only support of my widowed mother. Returning from three years' service in France, I borrowed some of her savings and got married." He explained that after losing his job in Edmonton, he had to leave his family behind. "My object in pulling off this job was to get money to settle my debts and pay back my mother."

Purvis pleaded with the judge as once he had pleaded with the police officer who had arrested him.

Back at the train station in the moments before his arrest, Purvis had made Detective Van Gorder an offer. "How much would you take to call it square?" he asked. "Let me catch the train."

He had missed that ride. But now the judge ensured the confessed train robber caught another. He sentenced Purvis to eight years' hard labour in the Prince Albert Penitentiary. Purvis left that night under escort, taking the same route that would have carried him to freedom days earlier had the detective not derailed his plans.

MORE THAN VIOLENCE

I t was a cold night in early March. Though spring would be coming soon, there was still no hint of warmth in the air, only the kind of cold that cuts straight through you and chills you to the bone. Amanda was walking alone in Regina's inner city, hurrying along the deserted street with her slight frame braced against the icy wind.

She saw him at the intersection of 13th and Osler. She had seen him around before, and when he asked her where she was going, she stopped to talk to him for a minute. He was a friendly, easy-going guy, chatty and not bad looking. It was far too cold to be standing outside talking, so when he invited her to his place to have a drink and warm up, Amanda immediately said yes.

They walked together to his room at the Salvation Army, just a few blocks away. His small apartment was tidy and comfortable, and Amanda settled in while he poured her a stiff rye and Pepsi. They were sitting together talking about everyday things, like life and the weather, when Amanda started to feel woozy. Then there was blackness and searing pain.

It was nearly six in the morning when he carried Amanda outside and left her in the back alley. She was soaking wet and barely conscious, and had been lying in his bathtub for almost seven hours by then, drifting in and out of consciousness as blood flowed from two cuts deep inside. He shoved some paper towel down her pants before he hauled her out, dropping her against a dumpster in the pre-dawn cold. As he walked back into the Salvation Army, he told a couple of staff members there was a drunk passed out in the alley.

* * *

Although she was still a young woman by the time she met Randy Burgmann on a Regina street in March of 2004, Amanda had already lived a long and difficult life. She had grown up surrounded by violence and abuse of all kinds, and had been repeatedly molested by her cousin Duane as a child. Amanda's sister, Michelle, later stabbed Duane to death. Michelle went to jail for it, got four and a half years for manslaughter. That's the only part of Duane's death Amanda really felt bad about.

Amanda headed out on her own when she was still a child, trading the violence and abuse at home for more of it on the street from strangers. At 30, she had seven children, none of whom lived with her. She was also a longtime drug addict and alcoholic, had Hepatitis C, and was often malnourished and anemic.

But despite her many problems, on the evening of March 11, 2004, Amanda was feeling pretty good. She spent the day drinking at her mother's house in Regina with a small group of relatives and friends, sharing four or five big cans of cheap, high-alcohol beer among five people, then splitting some injection drugs with her mother. As the evening went on Amanda wanted to drink more, but had no money to buy alcohol. In this way, she had been happy to run into Randy Burgmann.

Amanda finally emerged from the darkness to find herself in the hospital. She had nearly died, and had received a blood transfusion and needed surgery to repair the cuts inside her vagina. She checked herself out of the hospital a few days later.

As police continued to look for a suspect in the brutal assault, Randy sat down with a journalism student, Hiromi

Fusano, to talk about the problems ex-convicts, particularly sex offenders, face as they try to re-integrate into the community.

"My past is my past and I don't need it to keep on harming me," he told Fusano, sipping a cup of coffee and chatting casually with the young woman, who was videotaping the conversation for a school project.

During the interview, Burgmann told Fusano he was "99.9% sure" he wouldn't commit any more crimes in his life.

"I have no desire to go out and hurt another person emotionally or physically...," he said. "It happens, but it's not done intentionally."

The police arrested Randy a week later and charged him with aggravated sexual assault for the attack on Amanda.

* * *

Burgmann went to trial at Regina Court of Queen's Bench the next winter. The trial started on January 24, 2005, in front of a jury. Reporters filled the seats at the front of the courtroom to cover the proceedings. The case had made headlines not only because of the nature of the vicious assault, but because Burgmann had a history of violent sex offences against women. Police in Edmonton had even taken the rare step of releasing a public notice when Burgmann got out of prison, warning the public that they believed Burgmann posed a "risk of significant harm" to the community. Regina police didn't issue such a warning when he decided to move there instead.

Amanda was the first to testify at the trial, shyly telling a courtroom full of people what had happened to her in Randy Burgmann's apartment ten months earlier. She had already faced him once before, at his preliminary hearing, but it was different to tell the story in court. She was uncomfortable and embarrassed as the jury, the lawyers and the media stared at her and she was forced to lay bare the details of her problems, her past, and her injuries.

"I was all cut up inside," she testified.

As soon as she was finished, she fled the courtroom with her head down.

On the second day of the trial, Justice Ted Malone came into the courtroom looking grim. He told those in court he was forced to declare a mistrial in the case, because a television newscast had mentioned Burgmann's past sexual assault convictions. In most jury trials, the accused's criminal history is kept from the jurors so it cannot prejudice their decisions.

With no other option, Malone dismissed the jury and adjourned the case for two months.

The trial began anew before a different jury in March. Once again, Amanda faced Randy Burgmann from the stand. Again, she told the judge, the lawyers, the media and twelve jurors about meeting Burgmann on the street, about going to his room for a drink and then sliding into darkness and pain.

"I remember it being dark and I was asking him to stop...," she said. "He was hurting me down below."

Burgmann stared at Amanda while she testified, but she looked down, not meeting his eyes or those of the jurors who would decide his fate.

In police interviews that were played for the jury during the trial, Burgmann at first denied any involvement with Amanda, but later admitted he'd let her into his apartment to warm up. He told investigators Amanda had gotten "frisky, " and said he was "playing around" when he injured her accidentally. Burgmann said he didn't even know anything was wrong until he saw that his hand was covered in blood, then panicked because he knew he would be judged by his past offences.

"It doesn't matter what I say," he told one police officer. "I'm an ex-con being charged."

In his closing argument to the jury, defence lawyer Bruce Campbell argued the injuries happened in the course of "vigorous consensual sexual intercourse," and attributed the severity of Amanda's wounds to her fragile health.

"These two people met, they had sex and she was injured," he said. "If that occurred in lawful conduct, it's not a crime."

But Crown prosecutor Jeff Kalmakoff said Amanda did not consent to sexual activity, and could not have consented to the injuries she received.

"Have you ever had consensual sex that required surgery?" he asked the jury. "Have you ever had consensual sex that required hospitalization?"

Jurors deliberated for seven hours before sending out a letter indicating they could not reach a consensus. It was a hung jury. When Justice Malone asked whether the jurors wanted more time to consider the matter, the jury foreman said no.

Randy Burgmann, March 7, 2005, photographer Melanie Schoenthaler, courtesy *Regina Leader-Post.*

"We don't feel we'd be able to reach a decision, Your Honour," he said.

The jury was dismissed, and plans were set in motion for a third trial.

Six months later, in September 2005, Burgmann and Amanda met again in the same courtroom before a new judge and new jurors. Though it had been a somber affair from the beginning, the mood now was even more serious. The stakes were getting higher, and both sides knew that another hung jury—or an acquittal—was possible.

Amanda was emotional as she testified against Burgmann once again.

"He hurt me. He raped me. The evidence is all there," she said. "I didn't have consensual sex. When someone consents to sex you don't get hurt and cut up inside."

The trial lasted four days, with both sides restating their arguments. This time, the jury deliberated little more than two hours before reaching a decision. The room was tense as the jurors filed back to their seats, and Justice Catherine Dawson asked the foreman if they had reached a verdict. They had: Randy Burgmann was guilty of aggravated sexual assault.

Outside court, prosecutor Jeff Kalmakoff lauded the verdict, and particularly what it would mean for Amanda.

"Hopefully this is the end of the road for her in terms of having to come back to court and deal with this case," he said. "Hopefully it's over and done with and I'm sure she'll be relieved if that's the end of it."

The Crown immediately began an application to have Burgmann declared a dangerous offender. The designation is intended for the country's worst criminals, and is more severe than a life sentence since it involves an indefinite term of imprisonment with only periodic reviews. At that hearing, unlike his trial, Burgmann's past crimes would play a key role.

* * *

Randy Burgmann was 26 when he broke into his ex-girlfriend's house in Edmonton in the summer of 1989, angry at the woman because he believed she was playing mind games with him.

"The only thing going through my head was to snap her neck," he would later recall.

He beat the woman viciously, dragging her around the room and banging her head against the wall while telling her he was going to rape her. He would remember his blood "curdling with hate" during the attack.

Burgmann was arrested and charged.

While out on bail, he went to visit the girlfriend of a co-worker. He asked the woman to have sex, and when she said no, he raped her and beat her until he was too exhausted to continue. The woman's children were waiting outside the door of the house at the time. Burgmann would later describe the assault as "pure violence," and said the sex was "basically just a bonus." He was sentenced to ten months in jail for the attack on his ex-girlfriend, and four and a half years for the rape. He was out of jail by the end of 1994.

On New Year's Eve, soon after his release from prison, Burgmann picked up a prostitute in Edmonton and beat and raped her brutally before throwing her out of his truck onto the street. He picked up another woman a few hours later and embarked on another violent attack, kicking the woman, pulling out clumps of her hair, and driving her outside the city before she was able to jump out of his truck and run naked to another car for help.

Writing about the attacks later for a prison counselling program, Burgmann remembered feeling powerful and "God-like" and thinking: "This bitch is going to die. She needs to be humiliated badly. She is going to pay for what she did."

He was sentenced to nine years in prison for the New Year's Eve attacks.

"This was strictly nothing more than violence," Burgmann admitted, talking to Regina police sergeant Murray Walton about the attacks years later for a police training video. "I was going to kill her."

Asked by Walton why he didn't, Burgmann said: "She escaped."

Randy Burgmann moved to Regina after being released from prison in 2001, and was in the city for eight months before he breached his parole and was taken back into custody. After that, he was held to the very end of his sentence, which expired in January 2004. He met Amanda on the street six weeks later.

During his years in prison, Burgmann had taken extensive counselling, and had excelled in even the most intensive programs for sexual and violent offenders. He could talk about his offences and the impact on his victims in a way that impressed even the experts, and he was described in many prison reports as intelligent and well-spoken. Many of the parole officers, correctional officers, and other prison employees who met him found him charming and likeable. Forensic psychiatrist Dr. Shabehram Lohrasbe was one of the few not convinced by Burgmann's charm.

"I found him to be hollow in emotion. He would talk about things, but it was an emotional vacuum ...," Dr. Lohrasbe testified at Burgmann's dangerous offender hearing. "I was struck by the fact that he didn't seem to have any emotion even when he was talking about himself.

"He doesn't seem to be a man who's really searching or really troubled by what's going on inside him."

The sentiment echoed the feelings of another expert, psychologist Elise Reeh, who had told court: "He knows how much the victim suffers and yet he still chooses to do it."

The roots of Burgmann's behaviour are unclear. He claims he was viciously sexually abused by two women as a very young child, and then abused physically by others in his life. He has also given a variety of accounts of time in the military, though many of his claims are hard to verify.

What is known is that Burgmann admits to having fantasies about killing women, and shows signs of sadism and sexual sadism.

In his interview with Sergeant Walton, conducted a month before the attack on Amanda, Burgmann said there is one thing most people didn't understand about him and his offences.

"It's not about the sex," he told Walton. "If people could actually get past the sex part, they would see what kind of offender I am."

* * *

On March 11, 2008, just one day less than four years after they first crossed paths on a cold and empty street, Amanda and Randy met one last time in a Regina courtroom. Burgmann sat glowering in the prisoner's box. The 45-year-old looked tired and angry.

Justice Catherine Dawson, who had reviewed thousands of pages of evidence, listened to weeks of testimony and considered the matter for several months, said she believed Burgmann's prospects for rehabilitation were "nothing more than hope." Reading aloud from a lengthy written decision, Dawson said it was interesting that so many people who had worked with Burgmann were convinced he could change, and she speculated he was either unable to change his ways, or a master of manipulation.

"Or perhaps both," she added.

Dawson declared Randy Burgmann a dangerous offender, and he was led from the courtroom in shackles. Amanda, who had been sitting quietly on a bench at the back of the courtroom, slipped out without a word. She walked down the hall and out of the building, and headed into the cool March air.

The names Amanda, Michelle and Duane are pseudonyms, and have all been changed to protect the identity of the victim.

RING AND RUN

For a man who had been sleeping seconds earlier, Horst Hamm showed remarkable agility as he raced down from the third floor and grabbed the phone before it rang a third time. He was hoping to reach it before anyone else awoke.

Standing by the stairs on the second floor with the phone in hand, he looked to the south and noticed the window glowing, as though someone had left a light on next door.

"Horst, the house next to yours is on fire," said the caller. Much later, Horst would remember that familiar female voice was surprisingly calm. But at that moment, his only thoughts were for his wife and three sons sleeping on the third floor. He slammed down the phone and headed back upstairs, yelling as he ran. "Fire!"

The glare through the window was growing in intensity.

Suspecting some sort of family emergency had sparked the late-night call, Jane Hamm had stood listening at the entrance to the bedroom when her husband went to get the phone. Dressed in her nightgown, she was struck by how extremely warm she felt on this winter night. There was only one heating duct on the third floor of the Victorian-era home, so all of the beds had heavy feather ticks that had been made by Horst's mother. With her back to the window as she stood in the doorway, Jane was oblivious to the inferno building outside—

Fire rages through three properties in Regina on Dec. 5, 1990. Joyce Metz was later convicted of arson. Photo courtesy Regina Fire Department.

until she heard her husband. Then she turned and took in the massive wall of flames outside the window.

Suddenly everything was lit up like a stadium.

"There's a fire next door. We've got to get out of the house," Horst shouted, reaching for their youngest, who had earlier crawled into his parents' bed. The groggy 6-year-old fell back asleep. Horst grabbed the child, dragging him into the hall, and screaming again that they had to get out. The other two boys, aged 9 and 11, came out of their bedroom with Jane right behind. There were three smoke detectors in the house, but not one was going off. Despite the intense heat, there was still no smoke.

"Run downstairs and don't stop until you're out on the street," Horst ordered as he stuffed some of the clothes discarded on the floor a few hours earlier into his sons' arms. He stopped to pull on his own pants.

In the stairwell, Jane saw that the walls had taken on an orange glow. The window facing the neighbour's house to the south was rippling, like waves on a river. The window was melting. But that was inside.

Outside on this December 5 night in 1990, strong, bitter winds easily carried the flames to the Hamms' Regina house and chilled the now-homeless family. Once her children were safely out the door, Jane grabbed coats from the front closet and threw them to the porch to passers-by, who had seen the flames and come to help. In shock, she turned back inside to get boots from the back door as she thought about her sons' bare feet on the frigid pavement. Jane could hear the creaking and roaring of the fire as she passed through her kitchen. She didn't stop until she got outside to the garage. She turned and started to scream for her husband, thinking he was going to die inside the fire that was quickly consuming their home of fourteen years.

Horst had lost sight of his wife and sons. Standing alone on the second floor, he noticed the flames had found their way inside. He made it to the main floor in time to see Jane flee out the back door. But where were the children? Terrified to leave without them, he ran through the main floor to the back door and saw Jane, clad only in her nightgown and clutching boots in her hands. "Get out of the house Horst," she screamed, as parts of it were falling down around them.

"Where are the kids?" he replied. He hurried through what was left of the main floor, spotted his sons outside at the front of the house, and stepped off the front porch to join his family. The windows overhead were blowing out as a result of the intense heat.

Standing safely with his children, Horst looked across Retallack Street at his house. The roof line had collapsed. The third floor, where they had been sleeping, was now part of the second.

Two or three minutes had passed since that phone call. "In retrospect, putting on my pants was probably a big mistake. There was no real time to spare," Horst would say later when reflecting on those frantic moments.

* * *

Joan Carol Orazewska also got a phone call that night.

It came too late to wake her.

Unable to make it through the late-night news, she had climbed into bed in the second-floor office above her store around 11:10 p.m. The cat she had recently adopted from the Regina Humane Society woke her more than two hours later with its meowing. That's when Joan heard the loud crackling, the exploding glass crashing, and the whipping wind. The room was illuminated.

She knew there was no time to do anything but run like hell. As Joan passed the bathroom on the second floor, she caught sight of the flames through the window. She couldn't tell where one building began and the other ended or, for that matter, exactly whose house was burning. But she knew to keep running down the winding staircase of the three-storey building.

The picture window in the hall exploded just as she cleared the second-floor landing. A second longer, and Joan may well have not made it down those stairs. Reaching the main floor, she bolted through the living room and kitchen and headed to the back door. The ringing telephone stopped her. Joan took a step back inside and answered. Struggling to find her voice, she could manage only to stammer hysterically, "Help, get help." Joan recognized the voice on the other end. It was her neighbour, who calmly told Joan there was a fire.

Joan dropped the phone and ran.

From the fire hall three blocks away, firefighters could see the smoke and flames shooting skyward. First to arrive at 2075 Retallack Street, Captain John Turner felt like he was looking into a furnace, glowing red hot. The two-and-a-half storey house had been burning so long it resembled an ember that would crumble if touched. He radioed for the pump company to catch a hydrant. The flames, fanned by thirty-kilometre winds, were licking at the Hamms' house next door at 2071.

Around the corner on 13th Avenue, fire was rolling over the roof of Joan's unique little gift shop, the Wicker Basket. The northwest wind was creating a vortex between the buildings, drawing in the flames. The intense heat sent not just embers, but full chunks of roof a block away. When the wind shifted, the fire raged even worse and there were fears it would spread further to the Cathedral area's older homes. It took twenty-six men from the Regina Fire Department more than five hours to keep that from happening.

Located on the same block on 13th Avenue was the Campbell and Haliburton insurance sales office. When Brent Gibson arrived for work that morning and saw the destruction across the street, he dug out the file he had prepared less than a month earlier. He phoned in an insurance claim for his customer, Joyce Metz.

* * *

On the first of every month, Brent and Charlotte Smith had paid their landlady almost $500 for the three-bedroom house at 2075 Retallack Street. On her own since age 15, Joyce Metz owned her first property—with clear title she would proudly proclaim—within three years. By the time she was 60, she owned fifteen properties, including the Retallack Street house.

It was a bit of an eyesore when the Smiths moved in. Just that summer in 1990, Joyce had the eavestroughs fixed and the basement wall reinforced. The wall was caving in from a leaky water heater. The contractors had suggested excavating around the entire exterior and laying a retainer wall. Instead, Joyce found a cheaper fix.

The Smiths gave Joyce their notice at the end of October, so Brent could take a job out east. In the month before they actually moved out, the couple noticed the raspberry bushes in the backyard had been uprooted by Joyce, and sold or given away to her friends and acquaintances. It seemed odd, given her apparent affinity for the shrubs. When the Smiths moved in, the rental agreement held them responsible for tending to the raspberries, although they were forbidden from eating any of the fruit. When they pointed out the inherent unfairness in the arrangement, Joyce agreed they could share the fruit but only she could pick it. She later relented and allowed them to pick their own—to subsequently accuse them of taking too much. The Smiths were surprised when the contentious raspberry bushes and the apple tree, with its limbs extending towards Joyce's 13th Avenue property that backed the rental house, disappeared in November.

That was not the only surprise.

The Smiths had been asking their landlady to put in a smoke detector since they moved in, but she insisted it was their own responsibility. Suddenly in November, Joyce and a friend put a smoke detector in the kitchen (near the half-bathroom where the pipes stuck out from the wall waiting for faucets that were never installed).

During that month, Joyce phoned several times to ask when they would be out of the house because she had "arrangements" to make.

Those arrangements included dropping by Campbell and Haliburton where Joyce signed a policy upping the insurance on 2075 Retallack from $28,000 to $90,000 replacement value. She also added $5,000 contents insurance. The policy took effect November 8, less than a month before the fire.

Joyce was interested in renovating her 13th Avenue property, a large, two-storey brick building next to the Wicker Basket, to create a duplex with retail space on the bottom and residential above—until she discovered there wasn't enough parking to accommodate her plans. The contractor had given Joyce a quote of $140,000, including $4,500 to demolish the Retallack Street rental house. They met again on December 4. She suggested moving the house instead, to save money, but the contractor didn't think it stable enough. Joyce asked him to come back the next day, and they would look further.

He returned to find the smouldering ruins.

* * *

Siding salesman Robert Leonard Fleming fielded a call from Joyce in the summer of 1990. She wanted to know what it would cost to put siding on her 13th Avenue building. Joyce balked at the $16,000 estimate, and the middle-aged salesman said he'd try to do better. He found some cheaper siding, but she still thought the price too high.

Driving along 13th Avenue one day, Fleming stopped at Joyce's yard sale. He wondered if she had thought any more about getting her building sided, but Joyce still didn't like the price. "I'd rather burn it down," she told him.

"Well, we do that kind of work too," quipped Fleming. Later, on the witness stand, Fleming would swear he had been joking.

But somehow, there were further meetings. Joyce suggested she could go away for a weekend while he burned down her 13th Avenue property. But by October, Joyce had changed her mind. No longer did she want to burn down her house; she'd rather destroy her revenue property on Retallack. In early November 1990, she mentioned it would be nice to see the whole corner block taken out.

Fleming got a call after lunch on December 4 to meet Joyce. The house had to go immediately, she said. Joyce would help him "prepare" it. At Canadian Tire, Fleming bought a can of red spray paint, and fifteen-minute road flares—the three-pack.

Joyce unlocked the back door and grumbled that the former tenants should have left the house cleaner. On the north wall of the main floor and upstairs, Fleming spray-painted upside-down crosses, circles, and swastikas in red. He wanted investigators to think it was the work of vandals. Fleming would one day tell a jury he was determined the north side of the house would be untouched by the fire, because he didn't want it spreading to the Hamms.

Meanwhile, Joyce took newspapers apart page by page and stuffed them into cupboards, a deacon's bench by the stairs, and the broom closet. The pair leaned wooden planks together in a bonfire-like teepee behind the basement stairs. An old carpet was added to the heap before they broke a basement window to guarantee the fire would have plenty of oxygen.

When they had finished, Joyce closed the front door and locked it. Then Fleming kicked it in, like a burglar. Before walking away, they slipped a brick behind the door so it would stay closed.

The plan was for Fleming to dial Joyce's number from his cellphone inside his car and let it ring once before he entered the rental house. After he left, he would phone again, letting it ring once to let Joyce know the fire had started. "I wanted Joyce to be there to watch for flame so she could phone the people next door so there'd be no danger. She'd phone the fire department as soon as she seen flame," he would testify.

Fleming did return, using a small flashlight to find his way inside. He felt the heat almost immediately. Someone had turned the furnace up full blast. An old crimson, velour armchair now sat in the hallway. As he headed to the basement, Fleming stopped at the phone shelf to pick up his package of flares. Except now there were three packages—six more flares. Tearing open the package he had bought, he took two flares downstairs, lit one and stuffed it into the waiting bonfire. He put the second in the armchair before fleeing out the front door.

Fleming looked back as he walked towards his car parked on 13th Avenue. Smoke was already billowing out the broken basement window. He hit redial to connect with Joyce's number, pressed send, and let it ring once. Then he left, believing Joyce was watching and would soon summon help as planned.

Phone records indicate otherwise.

Fleming made the calls to Joyce's house at 12:41 a.m. and 12:49 a.m. Each lasted less than six seconds. Almost forty-five minutes passed before the Hamms and Joan next door got Joyce's calls. They escaped with their lives, but little else.

Meeting at a donut shop a week later, Joyce praised Fleming for his work.

"The car is yours," she told him, meaning a 1975 Austin Mini Minor worth $3,000 by Joyce's estimate. It was to be his down payment. An angry Fleming wondered how the fire had gotten so out of hand. Joyce assured him he had done Joan Carol a favour getting rid of her business, and that the people in the neighbouring house were welfare recipients. "You probably gave them the best Christmas present they ever had," she said, speaking of the outpouring of charity from people and businesses moved by the Hamms' plight.

In fact, the loss of her business was a devastating blow to Joan, and the Hamms were not on welfare. These were only two of several lies Joyce told.

Fleming had once promised Joyce he would go to the police if anyone was hurt. As the cops were moving in, he kept his word and cut a deal that would keep him out of jail. He pleaded guilty to conspiring with Joyce to burn down her rental house, and received a suspended sentence and probation. He was the star witness at Joyce's trial a year later.

Fleming was confronted on the witness stand with a December 15 receipt showing an $1,100-payment in full for the Austin. Fleming swore he had never seen the receipt before.

As well, private investigator Sandor Demeter testified that Joyce had offered him $5,000 if he would go to court and say he had heard Fleming tell her, "I can help you make some money." Demeter refused.

Joyce herself testified that Fleming had once bragged to her that he had burned down a house before, and shot and killed three men who had raped a friend's daughter. She was afraid of Fleming, she insisted. She never asked him to burn down her property, and only learned of the fire when she heard crackling and popping—which prompted her calls. When police had searched Metz's house fourteen days after the fire, officers found a piece of paper tucked into a book on a night table next to the phone. On it were the handwritten phone numbers for the Hamms and Joan.

Justice Ken Halvorson called Joyce unreliable, evasive, aggressive, unresponsive and contradictory. "To believe her evidence, I would have to disbelieve not only Fleming but at least six independent witnesses." The car receipt was as phoney as her story about Fleming, the judge decided. In truth, Joyce was the arsonist, motivated to collect insurance on her rental house rather than pay to fix the structural problems, he concluded.

Joyce Metz, Sept. 14, 1992, photographer Patrick Petit, courtesy *Regina Leader-Post.*

"But for a few seconds, the accused could have been facing constructive murder charges. It is difficult to envisage a situation where an arson could have come closer to causing deaths," Halvorson said. He sentenced Joyce Metz to six years in prison. An extra year was later added when she was convicted of perjury for lying while trying to get bail on the arson charges.

In dollars, the fire caused at least $400,000 in damage. The emotional toll on the victims couldn't be as easily quantified.

Joyce's insurance never did pay out—but it was only a setback for the woman who had worked her way up from virtually nothing. Even before she was charged, before the police closed in, Joyce began emptying bank accounts and selling off her properties. For the fire-sale price of $15,000, one man picked up the Retallack Street property that Joyce had insured for $90,000. The buyer was a firefighter from Vancouver. He was also related to Joyce. Her own 13th Avenue property was bought by her boyfriend—paid for mostly with a loan from Joyce's relative. When the civil suits from her victims and their insurance companies started rolling in, Joyce insisted she had nothing.

The courts weren't convinced, and ordered her to pay up.

In the year before the fire, Joyce had become friendlier towards her neighbour Joan. Perhaps they should pool their properties to make the parcel more attractive to buyers, Joyce had suggested. Joan wasn't interested. But Joyce was interested in Joan. She envied how the businesswoman had left 13th Avenue and lived on the West Coast, returning only at peak seasons to operate her store.

Joyce longed to sell everything and live in B.C., where things might be easier, the climate better, she told Joan.

When the civil trial was underway, Joyce never bothered to attend.

By then the parolee was living in Victoria, B.C.

THE PRISONER'S HEAD

J ohn took a seat at the table. He was a young man with a hearty appetite who liked a good meal, with plenty of meat, potatoes and bread with butter. Of late, he had often left this table dissatisfied. On this day, instead of a plate, he filled a piece of paper. His words spilled out, a man craving understanding. When he was hired six months earlier as a farm hand, he had agreed to work for one year. He would collect $18 a month and $20 extra for harvest. He had no quarrel with the money, but the second part of the agreement consumed him.

His English was not perfect, but the Hungarian immigrant had no trouble making his point. How could he work the long days expected by his employer, if he wasn't getting enough to eat?

"I was told you will get your meals with us, not a bit difference," John Mecsei wrote. "But they don't do that. They want to feed me with some scraps and fat meat and the tea just like water, and they try bake bread for me just like the soft grease. And they kicking at every meal, say the man eat too much. Well, I am 19 years old. Young fellow eat more what the 70 years age do."

Then John added: "Please Mr. J. Bruce Walker let me know what I can do with it because I cannot stand that treatment."

The letter was written on August 15, 1909, while John's employer was out. Five days later, J. Bruce Walker, commissioner of immigration at Winnipeg, sent his reply: "(I) would inform you that your employer is bound to give you sufficient wholesome food; he cannot make you work eighteen hours a day." He suggested John show his boss the letter. And if there was "any further trouble," he should take his concerns to the attorney-general in Regina.

John wrote Walker again five months later. In his tiny, careful penmanship, he composed his letter inside a Prince Albert prison cell. According to John, the letter from Immigration didn't sway his employers. It seems from their point of view, the problem wasn't a lack of food, but no shortage of appetite.

"I said, let me go or give me food," John explained. "The women told to me, 'How much do you want? A car load at a time? Never saw a dirty overloaded stomach like you eating too much.'"

The comments ate at John. He blamed them for driving him out of his mind. "If the men not in his mind, do not know and not understand what condition do anything and I went; then all at once Thoburn, his wife and his mother-in-law, three at a time, they are dead."

* * *

The bawling sound of hungry cattle prompted the Dixons to stop by their neighbours' farm. No one answered the couple's shouts or knocking at the locked door. Looking through the window, Ben and Catherine Dixon saw a little girl sitting by the stove. Mary was trying to warm her feet in the oven, except there was no heat. Someone must be around, they thought, calling out again. Mary, not yet 2 years old, wouldn't talk to them. The Dixons got back in their buggy and went to get help.

When they returned, Mary was standing at the kitchen window crying. Once inside the two-room house, they heard a noise and found her brother George Jr., days shy of his fourth birthday, in the potato cellar below the kitchen. He was alive. The same could not be said of his father.

The blinds were drawn in the bedroom, blocking out most of the afternoon's daylight. Near the door to a second cellar, someone had tried to wipe up something on the floor. Lifting the trap door, neighbours found George Thoburn Sr., dressed in his work clothes, lying head first in the hole. His feet rested against the trap door. The shot to his right shoulder had fractured ribs, collapsed a lung and struck a large blood vessel. The 34-year-old veteran of the Boer War and former train engineer had bled to death.

Neighbours reported the discovery to law officials before heading home to dinner.

Several hours passed before the other bodies were found. Barbara, Thoburn's wife of five years, was about a quarter-mile from the house. She was noticeably pregnant with her third child. Her 70-year-old mother Mary McNiven, lying in the bluff, was even more difficult to find. After her husband's death three years earlier in Ontario, she had moved to Saskatchewan to be closer to her two daughters.

There was no sign of John Mecsei, the hired man who had come to work on the Thoburn's farm, about three miles southwest of Clair. He wouldn't be found until the next day after searchers got word that he had stopped for dinner at a farm on the way to Wynyard. Mecsei was watering his horses when the posse caught up to him. A lynch mob waited for him by the hotel in Quill Lake after his arrest. But their appetite for revenge would not be filled that day.

* * *

John—or Jonas as his mother called him—had been working in the coal mines in Illinois, but opted to head to the Canadian Prairies and hire on as a farm labourer until he could file his own homestead claim. By all accounts, he was a good worker, although some of the neighbours noticed John was a little hard on the livestock, unsparing with the whip. "Everybody gets angry with oxen," Thoburn's neighbour Charles Baldwin explained.

He also remembered John griping about his meals.

At the start, John got along with the Thoburns and had no quarrel with the food. In John's mind, that all changed with Mrs. McNiven's arrival from Wadena. John overheard her complaining to her son-in-law that the new hired hand was eating too much.

John took it up with Mr. Thoburn, saying he couldn't stand the women talking to him that way. His boss promised it would stop, and it did. Mrs. McNiven went back home, and things seemed to improve.

Unfortunately, it didn't last.

"Mrs. McNiven came back from Wadena second week of July. She started her same story about me eating too much and not doing enough work," John claimed.

The food fights worsened. The Thoburns complained about John reaching for seconds. John insisted the meat was all fat and the soup thin.

On the night of October 31, John listened from his bed in the kitchen to the conversation coming from the next room. John had wanted to head to town the next morning to file for his homestead, but Mr. Thoburn had said the trip would have to wait until after freeze-up. Now, he was certain he heard Mrs. McNiven grumbling about him again. And her son-in-law seemed to be agreeing. John put the pillow over his head, trying to block out the conversation and the pain that was building. It felt like someone had stuck a needle into his head.

* * *

John awoke to a child's voice around noon.

"John shot papa to death," George Jr. was saying to no one in particular. "Mama went to Morley to get a doctor. John was going the way mama was going and mama was going away from John."

Stepping outside, John saw the horse, bridled and sweating, standing by the haystack. Back inside, George Jr. continued talking: "John was going to the stable, and the axe was in his hand."

"John shot papa to death," the boy repeated. John would later tell a courtroom that he found Mr. Thoburn in the cellar, and the two women outside.

"When I saw the women and saw the horse and see the marks on my pants and see the footmarks of my horse, it must have been I did it. I don't know the length of time I was going like that.

"I did not know I was doing this thing."

But the jurors seemed more convinced by the statement he had given upon his arrest. The one where he complained about not getting enough to eat, and told how he had shot Mr. Thoburn outside with the man's own shotgun before breakfast. Afterwards, John waited and watched from the stable for anyone coming out. When Mrs. Thoburn ran from the front door, John rode a horse ahead of her. He forced the 30-year-old woman to the ground, slit her throat with a butcher knife, and left her body in the scrub bush.

Finally, Mrs. McNiven stepped out. "Where are you John?" she asked, before running back inside. When she exited a second time, John clubbed her twice in the head with the barrel of the gun, breaking the stock.

John rode away with the Thoburns' horses and wagon, a coat, feed oats, blankets—and food.

He told the Mounties he had fed the children before leaving. They dined on cream cake, bread and butter, and meat.

At least, that's what he said.

When the neighbours found the two orphaned children a day later, they noticed the table was set—but only for one.

While the taking of three lives over too few slices of bread or not enough potatoes seemed mad, not one doctor would swear John was insane.

His mother Maria, living in Cleveland, Ohio, pleaded in a letter to the Hungarian Embassy to intervene so her only son's life could be spared. She spoke of a family history of insanity. John's father had spent time in an asylum in Hungary before he became a vagabond. Maria had left Hungary in 1902 so she could work to support her three children, and sent for John three years later. The Austro-Hungarian Embassy, the Canadian Hungarian Brotherhood and the editor of the *Canadian Hungarian Farmer* sent letters pleading for clemency for her son.

And, never starved for words, John himself wrote.

His rambling letter, scrawled across sixteen pages, repeated his claims about food and work and his sick mind. "I did not want to kill that family with clear head ... I'm very sorry for it. I did not cry very much but I feelling [*sic*] in my heart very, very, very sorry. Yours Very Truly, John Mecsei."

The hunger pains that had knotted John's stomach and kept him awake at night on the Thoburn farm were not a problem at the jail. He gained weight waiting for his date with the hangman. At 8 a.m. on March 10, 1910, a knot of a different kind proved his undoing, following a breakfast that included dainties as a treat for the condemned man.

Some sort of mix-up on the gallows in Prince Albert left him swinging for a full thirteen minutes and five seconds before death ensued. He died from a slow strangulation rather than a quick broken neck.

Though they wouldn't certify him insane, doctors who hungered to learn more about John were calling for his head—even before the trap door swung.

Shortly before John's execution, his defence lawyer wrote to the federal justice minister: "I have been asked if after death it would be possible to obtain prisoner's head so as an examination of his brain might be made and scientific data furnished... Would it be possible to have the head shipped to me or to such doctor as I would advise in Saskatoon? This will probably appear a peculiar request, but the medical people felt so on the subject and in the interests of science, I thought I should make it."

FROZEN ASSETS

"The administration of justice is a search for the truth."
—Justice Gene Maurice at the sentencing of Tony Chin

The smell of greasy hamburgers and fries competed with the sweet aroma of Chinese food, a west-versus-east clash of cultures. The lunch rush had ended an hour earlier, and the staff were finally getting a bite to eat themselves when Constable Ross Burton and his partner walked into the Swift Current restaurant. They were directed to an office at the rear of the building and found the owner, David Tam, sitting behind his desk, chatting with a salesman. His good friend Tony Chin, dressed in cook's clothes, was nearby, eating a plate of food. When the officers said they were there to see David, the other two men made a quick exit. David rose to shut the door behind them.

"What's this about?" he asked.

"It's regarding sexual assaults," Burton replied. David was under arrest. The man who had spent the last thirteen of his thirty-seven years building his life, his business and reputation in this country sagged in his office chair. His head dropped to his chest. As Burton led his prisoner out through the restaurant, David said something to Tony, who was standing at the grill. At least, that's who Burton thought those words were directed at; David would later insist he was speaking to his wife. The words were in a foreign language; Burton had no idea what was said. The Mountie took his man by the arm and steered him towards the unmarked police car.

Back at the detachment office that afternoon on June 20, 1989, Burton asked David if he understood why he was there and explained again that he was accused of sexually assaulting children—Tony Chin's daughters to be exact; the man working in David's restaurant; the man he once considered one of his closest and trusted friends.

"We know everything. The girls told us everything. It's over. Understand?" said Burton. David gave a nod, which the officer took as a "yes." He asked David for a statement. "All I want is the truth. This is for the court, so it has to be the truth."

Burton would recollect the exchange nine months later as a witness at David's trial. He said that when he asked David how many times he had touched the girls, the answer was "just once." Burton challenged him, saying the girls were telling police it had been going on for years. "I just washed them" or "watched them"—Burton couldn't be sure which word David had used. "It was either 'washed' or 'watched.' "

Flipping through the girl's statements like a deck of cards, the officer told the accused, "We know exactly what you did."

"I just take them and show them movies, you know, then they want me to show them things," Burton quoted David as telling him. Burton repeated again that he knew what David had done, and listed a litany of allegations. The officer used his hands to simulate masturbation, making it clear what he was talking about. David asked to see his lawyer.

That's how the constable recalled that encounter.

David remembered it quite differently.

"He come to the restaurant an' then tell me something to do, and say me sex for some girl. I said, 'no.' " David said when the officer grabbed hold of his arm, he told him, "I no want go because I'm not do something to anybody," he testified before Justice Theodore Geatros.

David said the officer seemed to get angry when he was unable to answer his questions, which he couldn't understand because he had a better command of Cantonese than English. "He say, 'You sexed the girl.' I said, 'I never sexed the girl.'"

Trying to convince the judge of his innocence, David believed he knew what had motivated the charges: gold and greed.

David said he had entrusted Tony Chin to take care of his restaurant and his savings, sixty-four ounces of gold coins and wafers then worth about $40,000. Tony was to safeguard the small fortune in his home in February 1989 while the Tams took a trip to Hong Kong. David and his wife brought presents of necklaces for the Chin children on their return three weeks later. But Tony would not give him back his gold, and instead wanted David to go into business with him. Despite repeated requests, David never recovered the gold. Then the sexual assault charges arose.

David and his wife suggested the Chin children were pawns of their physically abusive father, who would do anything to keep his hands on David's gold.

Tony was never asked about the gold at the trial. But he had been when he took the witness stand for the prosecution at the preliminary hearing five months earlier; he swore he knew nothing about it.

His two daughters, age 12 and 8, told the court David had molested them and their two younger sisters, who never testified. They said they were lured with candy and money, and the incidents had occurred several times over the years, when their parents weren't home. When each, in turn, was asked exactly what had happened, they replied, "Intercourse." Pressed for more detail, one girl said, "He put the penis in the vagina," echoing the earlier testimony of her younger sister who said, "The dinky go in the vagina."

Citing credibility as the key, the judge said he believed the girls and convicted David of four counts of sexual assault. The sentence was two and a half years in prison.

David tried to appeal to a higher court, and failed.

He maintained his innocence—as did Tony Chin, who insisted he knew nothing about any stolen gold. After David went to jail, Tony himself became a restaurateur, operating his own leased business.

Released in 1991 from the Prince Albert penitentiary, David, the former prisoner, stepped up efforts to also liberate his fortune. He pressed the Mounties, who searched the Chins' house and found nothing.

On his lawyer's advice, David offered a ransom for his stolen gold. A meeting was arranged for the morning of January 19, 1993, in a downtown parking lot, but Tony never showed because of a mix-up in times. Another meeting was hastily arranged for that afternoon. David handed over $3,800—twenty-two $50s and twenty-seven $100s in marked bills. According to David, it was far less than the $10,000 Chin originally demanded.

David's money bought him a white plastic bag. It contained a solid block of ice. Suspended in the frozen mass were the gold coins and wafers David hadn't seen in four years.

The exchange was already in progress when an RCMP officer, who had helped arrange the sting operation, showed up. Still, he saw enough. When the Mounties caught up to Tony, he had the marked bills in his pocket.

This time, it was Tony who went on trial. The 36-year-old had juggled two and often three jobs so he could buy a home, raise his family and support other relatives since coming to Canada twelve years earlier from Vietnam. Now he was charged with theft and perjury, accused of lying about the gold when he swore to tell the truth at David's preliminary hearing.

Tony contended it was all a mistake, a mix-up by the interpreter who translated his testimony into English. He said he was being framed, and he had found the $3,800 on the floor of his garage.

The prosecution argued Chin's motive was pure greed for pure gold.

A jury agreed. His sentence, originally three months, was later doubled by the Saskatchewan Court of Appeal, which stressed the importance of honesty in protecting the integrity of the administration of justice.

Tony continued to maintain his innocence.

Perhaps the true innocents were the children—either dupes manipulated by their father out of greed, or precious youngsters whose childhood was marred by sexual abuse.

Before the allegations, David used to spend hours at the Chins' house playing mah jong. When Tony Chin added a son to his family after a string of daughters, David and his wife, who had no children, closed down their restaurant and threw a party for eighty people to welcome the boy. The Chin children appeared close to David, often calling him what sounded like "aback," a Chinese term meaning older brother, uncle. Staff remembered the children coming to the restaurant often, and David giving them free hamburgers, fries, candies and chocolate bars.

As one witness recalled at David's trial: "He treated them like gold."

Tony Chin is a pseudonym. A publication ban ordered by the court prohibits identifying him as it would disclose the identity of his daughters.

TIME BOMB

It was Monday morning and William Laqua was dressed in his Sunday best. He was playing records at the Gordon Neil Café when his ex-girlfriend, Beatrice Baragar, came downstairs and saw him beside the phonograph. Beatrice was not at all happy to find him there. Although the two had dated for years, she had recently grown tired of Bill, and had repeatedly made it clear that she no longer wanted anything to do with him. Laqua had even moved out of his room upstairs at the Gordon Neil Cafe, which was owned by Beatrice's grandmother, Mrs. Eri Lillie, and where Beatrice and her mother, Goldie, both lived.

Mrs. Lillie was out of town that day, and Beatrice and Goldie had just finished cleaning the dishes from the morning breakfast customers when Laqua arrived at the cafe. It was about 10:30.

With a population of just 236, there weren't many strangers in the town of Aneroid, and Laqua's situation was well known around the little community southwest of Moose Jaw. Everyone knew that Laqua had taken Beatrice to nearly every dance and party in the town for the last three years. It was also common knowledge that Laqua had repeatedly asked Beatrice to marry him, and that she had repeatedly turned him down. By the time Laqua walked into the Gordon Neil Cafe on the morning of December 3, 1928, everyone in town knew that Beatrice had, for the last three months, been seeing another suitor.

But though many in Aneroid were familiar with the details of his romantic life, few in town knew much else about Bill Laqua. The 35-year-old well digger kept largely to himself, and his past was somewhat of a mystery. Laqua spoke fluent German and was rumoured to have family in the U.S., but the thing for which he was known best was his use of explosives in well digging. The *Regina Daily Post* would later say that Laqua's skill with dynamite was "famed in the entire neighborhood."

There was other talk that would later find its way into newspaper reports, something about an "affliction of a morbidness which weakened the mind," though no details were ever given.

At 22, Beatrice Baragar was a large, heavy-set woman, with deep-set eyes and a long broad nose. She may not have been an ideal beauty, but to Bill, she was perfect and he adored her.

Seeing Bill in the café that day, Beatrice immediately asked him why he was wearing his good clothes. When he didn't answer, and perhaps sensing something strange in her former suitor, Beatrice ran upstairs, calling to her mother that she didn't want any visitors. Bill raced up the stairs after Beatrice and grabbed her before she could get into her room. As the two struggled, Beatrice screamed for her mother, and Goldie ran out into the hallway to help.

"You dirty dog, leave her alone," she shrieked at Laqua.

Beatrice's cousin, Adeline Wray, who had stopped by the café that morning to say hello, was downstairs when the commotion began. Hearing the women's cries, Wray ran upstairs but got only as far as the upper landing. She could see Bill down the hallway holding Beatrice close to him while she struggled to get free of his grasp. Goldie was standing just behind her daughter. Bill had a lit cigarette in his mouth and was holding a stick of dynamite in his hand. Wray watched as Bill lifted his hand and touched the stem of the dynamite to the lit cigarette. There was a sudden, blinding flash of light and a powerful explosion that shook the house and sent Wray toppling over the banister and downstairs.

Plaster was still falling from the walls and ceiling and the second storey of the building was filled with dense smoke when Wray crawled out into the street for help.

Constable Jack Grey was the first at the scene, but as he ran toward the house something landed in front of him and he stumbled on it, falling headlong to the ground. He realized he had tripped over a bloody body part.

* * *

It was just after two on a bitterly cold afternoon when *Regina Morning Leader* reporter Geoffrey Hewelcke boarded a Universal Airways Ltd. airplane, and lifted off from the Regina Aerodrome heading south. It was a frigid and uncomfortable flight, and immediately after the plane landed in Aneroid, Hewelcke rushed straight to the scene of the explosion. The carnage he found there was nearly impossible for him to describe.

"Laths and plaster spattered with blood and gruesome bits of human flesh covered the floor. Flesh and blood had sprayed against the south end of the hall. Great gouts of blood stained the wall at the north end," he wrote. "It seemed like nothing so much as a scene out of the battlefields of Flanders."

Standing in the hallway upstairs, Hewelcke saw that Beatrice Baragar's face had been completely torn off by the explosion, and that her arms were at opposite ends of the corridor. Bill Laqua's body was an even more gruesome sight, with his chest entirely torn out by the blast, and almost every bone in his head broken though the skin had stayed intact. Goldie's mangled body was in a bedroom off the corridor.

"It is, of course, presumed that the shock of the explosion was so violent that none of its victims felt any of the pains of death," Hewelcke wrote. "One of Laqua's arms has not been found. The undertakers and the police are still searching for it, with little chance of finding it for it is presumed that it and the hand which held the dynamite cartridge were blasted into nothingness."

Undertaker J. T. Hall traveled from Ponteix to Aneroid that afternoon, and quickly began collecting body parts at the grisly scene. Hewelcke marveled at the revolting task the undertaker faced.

"Somehow the scattered pieces were fitted together in three ghastly jigsaw puzzles and left in the dining room of the house covered by blankets," Hewelcke wrote.

It took nearly twelve hours to sort out the remains.

An RCMP constable checking Laqua's room at the Paris Cafe found a suitcase containing a stick of dynamite and three fuses. There were also two notes, each written on pages from a cheap pad of letter paper. One said: "My home address is Ida Laqua, Lake City, Minnesota." The other read: "My room rent is paid until the end of the month"

On top of the notes lay an old love letter from Beatrice and her photograph.

Laqua had copies of the same two notes in the breast pocket of his shirt, but they were bloody and nearly destroyed by the blast. Few other clues were found.

"An investigation made of his room in the Paris Cafe revealed few personal belongings beyond those which might have been picked up by any bachelor leading a semi-itinerant life such as his," Hewelcke wrote. "There were no letters from any members of his family, there were no pictures of the wife and children which are mentioned by current rumours."

Stories about Laqua's wealth also turned out to be unfounded, and police found less than $10 in his account at the Bank of Aneroid.

A coroner's jury was struck and heard evidence that afternoon. The jurors listened soberly to the testimony from Wray, who was the sole eye-witness to the explosion.

"Then they retired and consulted briefly, returning once

again with a verdict which laid the blame for the tragedy upon the love of Bill Laqua for a girl who would no longer have anything to do with him," Hewelcke wrote.

Hewelcke became so sick after the frigidly cold journey and his time at the gruesome crime scene that he was off work for ten days after filing his story that evening.

Two hundred people attended the women's funerals in Aneroid later that week. Mounds of flowers and wreaths covered the two caskets, which were then laid side by side in one grave at the Aneroid cemetery.

Laqua's sister, Ida, traveled from Minnesota to deal with her brother's remains, but she revealed nothing about his past and would not speak to reporters about what had occurred.

Only a handful of people attended Laqua's funeral service, and of those, none accompanied his remains to the cemetery. He was buried with barely a word, not far away from the women he killed.

BEGINNER'S LUCK

The craving gnawed at her throughout the day. Sometimes desire trumped control, and she stepped out during the lunch hour to satisfy the urge. But usually the middle-aged manager would wait until she got off work. Then Barbara could slip away to her favourite place for hours.

Expectations grew as she pulled out her money. With her hit, Barbara escaped in the blur of spinning images and melodious sounds—almost like a vision, if only for a few seconds. Sometimes, she could actually feel her heart rush under the adrenaline. The highs were incredible; the lows merely a setback.

She chased the highs.

At those times, an hour would pass in minutes, far away from the routine of work and family and stress. Here, in her second home, Barbara did not feel nearly so alone. When she walked into the room, she was somebody. She felt popular, a winner. Everybody knew her name. They welcomed her.

They welcomed her money most of all.

* * *

Timothy didn't notice when the cash began disappearing from his bank account. He had taken out a loan in June 1993 for $13,000. Three months later, he refinanced, and the debt grew to $17,700.

Eighteen days after Timothy refinanced, Mrs. Gutowski used the same Calgary bank for a $10,000 loan. She subsequently found it wasn't quite enough, so she topped it up a month later with a personal line of credit for $10,000. Terry Gutowski opened a chequing account and received a bank card to conveniently make withdrawals. Her address was a post office box number in Calgary.

James opened a $10,000 personal line of credit four days before Christmas in 1993. A month later, he needed a loan to pay for it. Getting in deeper, he refinanced through another loan come February. It wasn't long before the debt had grown to nearly three times what was originally borrowed.

The same could be said for Matt and Victor, who coincidentally had the same box number as Mrs. Gutowski. They also had trouble making their payments, yet their credit limits ballooned to $125,000 each.

In every instance, the loans had been created and approved by Barbara Ann Horvath. The trusted employee had risen in her fifteen years with the company, from a file clerk to a personal banking manager with sole authority to grant loans and credit. An audit while Horvath was on maternity leave raised concerns.

Corporate security officers visited the 35-year-old woman in March 1995. By then, Horvath had moved to Regina. They wanted to know about James, Victor and Matt and their debts, which totalled about $189,000.

"You're very familiar with some of these customers," suggested investigator Bill Prebushewski.

"I know the name of all of them," Horvath replied.

Prebushewski wanted to know if she could actually recall Victor sitting down in front of her to apply for his personal line of credit.

"Probably. I can't remember the exact date," said Horvath.

But Prebushewski soon tired of the game. "Why should we fish around and fish around and fish around? I wouldn't be here if I thought these customers got the money. I wouldn't be here if I didn't think that I could show that you obtained all of these monies." His questions became more pointed. "Is there a real James Gallagher?"

"Umhm," said Horvath, taking a gamble. "I did meet with him. I did talk to him on the phone."

Prebushewski called her bluff. "Well, Barb, did you obtain all the monies from these for your own purposes?"

Before answering, Horvath wanted to know what the chances were of bank authorities going to the police. "They won't look at repayment of any kind or some sort of a deal to stay out of publicity?"

Urging her co-operation, Prebushewski asked if any of the money remained. "And the bigger question is, is this all of it? Are there other accounts that we've not discovered?"

Horvath was hedging. "Okay, and that would look favourably upon me?" The investigator agreed to tell police if she was co-operative, but then quickly added that they were getting ahead of themselves. He wanted to know more about each loan.

"Okay. Okay. If you just hang on two seconds," replied Horvath. She left the dining room table and went to the living room.

"This is what you are looking for," she said on her return, handing over five banking cards. She admitted there were five people, not three, and the amount was closer to $200,000. Timothy was the first fraud, in June of 1993. Like Victor and Matt, he was an actual bank customer, but they knew nothing about the loans. Mrs. Gutowski and James were equally oblivious—but that's because they existed only in Horvath's mind and on the phoney bank documents she had drafted.

"Why?" Prebushewski wanted to know.

"I'm a compulsive gambler, and I don't even know how to begin to say that—I'm fully, fully, fully addicted to the VLTs. This is where every cent of this money has gone."

Horvath explained how the video lottery terminals are like a slot machine in Vegas. "There are bells and whistles, and—well the VLT is similar to that. It's an electronic screen that's—the thrill of hitting the button, and the thing spins, and you know, if you win, you get credits and—ah—just for the thrill of it." It was more words than she had strung together through most of the conversation.

"Have you ever walked out of there at night with profit in your pocket?" Prebushewski asked.

Horvath's answered with only two words: "No. Never."

She always remembered her first big win. It was on a Friday night, after work. She had gone for a few drinks at a Calgary hotel and ended up trying her luck at the recently installed video lottery terminals. Horvath walked away that night with a $1,000 jackpot.

But later there were many nights when she left with nothing. And too often her paycheques at the bank couldn't cover her after-hours obsession that was costing up to $1,000 a night, peaking at $10,000 a month. Often she left the bank at 3:30 in the afternoon and played the VLTs until 2 a.m. She was a high roller, always playing her maximum number of credits.

The deception didn't stop in Calgary or with Prebushewski's questions. Horvath applied nearly a year later for a $25,000 personal line of credit at a Regina bank. Well, actually, it was for her husband, Barbara explained, but he was too busy to take care of it himself. Banking staff allowed the personable Horvath to take the documents home and get them signed. She did the same at a Winnipeg bank two months later to increase the credit by $5,000. Her husband knew nothing of his forged signature or the bank's $35,581 loss.

After Horvath pleaded guilty to both crimes in November 1996, the courts took a gamble. Judge Eugene Lewchuk gave her a conditional sentence. Then on the law books only two months, the new penalty option allowed Horvath to serve nine months in the community, while she wore an electronic ankle bracelet, and the remaining fifteen months under conditions, including that she get some treatment.

According to an expert in gambling addictions, Horvath was pathological—9.5 on a scale of 10. ("I don't like putting anybody at 10," Don Ozga conceded as he testified at Horvath's sentencing hearing.) To him, having Horvath work at a bank was akin to an alcoholic minding a liquor store, since the VLTs were as addictive as crack cocaine. "These are not innocent machines," Ozga told the court.

Defence lawyer Bill Howe persuaded the judge to accept pathological gambling as a mental illness. "My friend (the prosecutor) says, 'Well, so what, if a person has a cocaine addiction and then goes to the bank and robs the bank, the court doesn't treat that person any differently than another person that might rob a bank.' The difference with that distinction is it's the government. It's the people themselves that have created the cocaine."

He told the judge Horvath was likely the first pathological gambler to come before the Saskatchewan courts, but he aptly predicted the odds were good more would follow. After her precedent-setting sentence was upheld by the province's highest court, many more wagered their gambling addiction should spare them from a jail cell—and won: a Saskatoon bookkeeper who embezzled $354,000 while employed by a veterinary teaching hospital; a civil servant who siphoned off $25,000 from the Social Services Department; and even the financial officer of a corporation operating casinos who bilked his employer of $66,000.

And they all had first-time offender Horvath to thank for leading the way.

But her beginner's luck ran out in 2001.

Horvath had found part-time work setting up displays in large Regina department stores. The same charm that had once allowed her to glean passwords from co-workers at the Calgary bank—so she could maintain her fake accounts while on maternity leave—kept store staff from checking out the parcels she carried from the businesses.

A police officer working the pawn shop detail recognized her name among the clients. Surveillance on May 29, 2000, showed Horvath arriving at a department store and leaving an hour later for the pawn shop. She collected $375 that day by hawking the pilfered goods, and spent the next two hours playing her favourite VLT—the third machine at a local restaurant, the one that had been her undoing five years earlier. She still had stolen loot in her car when she was arrested on July 21, 2000, at the same restaurant.

Over fifteen months, she had pawned 423 DVDs, 32 VHS movies, and 229 video games for Nintendo 64, Gameboy, Sony Playstation and Dreamcast. The affable Horvath told the pawn shop she was getting the items through the Internet and received freebies because of the volumes. She was convincing enough that the pawn shop handed over $16,000. The department stores were out $64,000 in merchandise.

But this time she had hit a losing streak. Gone was her family, her marriage, her job and her freedom. Like before, she was sentenced to two years less a day, except this time Horvath was to serve it in jail. The court also upped the ante with a three-year probation order that included a condition that any potential employer be alerted to her criminal record.

Horvath told police she felt so badly about stealing that she wanted to throw up—but when she was winning, gambling made her feel better.

DEAR JOYCE

"**D**ear Joyce," the love letter began.

The words filled both sides of a single sheet of paper. Written while the author was in a treatment centre in Saskatoon, the letter was dated October 3, 1990. "I still have dreams about you—you and me in building a life together. I love you and still want to marry you and also become a fatherly figure towards Bradley and Clinton."

The letter was signed, "Love A Friend, Garry C. Ganton."

Joyce Espedal kept the letter in a cupboard beside the fridge. It was there next to another, dated December 24, 1990.

"Joyce, I need help. I need it bad. I believe you are a friend. I have hurt you...," the letter began.

Garry continued to pour out his thoughts. "I also believe that I have to do something bad and I don't want to have to do that. I am telling you this not to scare you or threaten you, but to ask for advice... Please Joyce, be my friend and help me."

Adding "3:30 p.m." to the top, the 38-year-old wrote another letter to Joyce that very same day.

"I have a hard time understanding what you told me last weekend and that was, 'Garry, I care for you and don't want to see you get into any more trouble. So okay Garry, I can come to visit you, but if you come to visit me, the police got the neighbours watching and besides the law has got a restraining order saying you can't go to Joyce's.' So if you really care, why is it you never come to visit me?"

He also wrote to his mother that day. "I am sick, very sick... Henceforth, I feel like letting the law take its course, so fuck the world and everybody in it."

Ever since the car accident, when he was 17 and ended up in a coma for a couple weeks, Garry found it easier to put his thoughts down on paper than to speak them. There were other changes, too. He went from being generous and likable to intolerant and impulsive. His mood worsened when he drank. Garry started making lists after the brain injury, to help him remember things. Garry's list on the kitchen table reminded him on December 27, 1990, to go to the bank, to Social Services, to the service station, and to buy cigarettes and twenty-four cans of beer.

It's not clear exactly when Garry made the other to-do list. It was an undated single sheet of paper. The reminder lay in a plastic bag with some other papers, tucked into a corner at the end of the hallway in his Melfort apartment suite.

"Phone mum in the morning to let her know as to whether or not I can come for dinner. Also let her know that I need help, but I don't or don't want to know where to go," read the first entry on the list.

Next: "Go see Fernie tonight to borrow some cash to buy beer."

The final entry was the most concise: "Do Joyce in tonight."

* * *

The temperature on December 28, 1990, was a frigid -32°c when the Vanderbyls spotted the two boys near the side of the isolated road. The brothers, aged 3 and 4, were in the ditch fifteen kilometres northwest of Melfort, all alone. The older one had blood on his cheek. His younger brother was slipping into a coma. One had lost his toque and a boot. The other's hood was off. Neither had mittens. The 3-year-old would end up losing eight of his frostbitten fingers.

Although he was difficult to understand with his frozen face, the older boy managed a few words.

He wanted his mommy.

* * *

Garry's parents were sitting down to lunch when he walked into their home. His mother asked if he wanted to join them.

"I think you should call the police," Garry replied. "There's a dead body in my apartment."

His mother asked, "Who?"

His father guessed, "Joyce?"

Asked how it had happened, Garry held up his hand. "With this," he said. "I just reached in her throat."

When police arrived at his parents' home, Garry stretched out his arm with the key to his suite hanging from his fingertips. "There's a body in my apartment."

Police found Joyce Espedal lying on her back on the bedroom floor. She was nude from the waist down. Her 32-year-old face was covered in blood.

Two months earlier, Garry had been hauling scrap iron with a friend when they got talking over beers. Garry was upset about Joyce, accusing her of drinking too much and not looking after her children.

"If she doesn't straighten out ... I'll kill the bitch," Garry said. He made plans, too. Once, Garry had cut up plastic bags to cover his hands and feet. Another day, he had a rope ready to strangle her. And then there was the time they were having supper and he had a butcher knife sitting between them. He thought about stabbing her, but never followed through.

When Garry saw his probation officer on November 5, 1990, he told him how he had broken into Joyce's home the weekend before. He had beaten up and raped Joyce. Garry admitted that he had even considered strangling her to death. The probation officer personally drove Garry, a binge drinker, to an alcohol detox centre that same day, requested a psychiatric exam, and notified the RCMP.

Garry wrote to Joyce three weeks later. "I realize that I have been leaning pretty heavy on you. I even hurt you and I want to improve my behaviour. At the beginning of November something bad happened and I have been scared since because I did not know I could be that kind of person."

If she had not already realized it, Joyce would soon learn exactly what kind of person Garry could be.

Joyce walked into the hotel in Melfort around ten at night on December 27, 1990, to buy a dozen Molson Canadian beer. As the manager got Joyce's purchase, two young boys walked in, followed by Garry. He sat down at the bar and ordered a beer. The bartender explained that he couldn't serve Garry with his two young children present.

"They're not my fucking kids," Garry shot back.

"They're mine," said Joyce, and the boys followed her out. Garry finished his draught and left about two minutes later.

According to Garry, they ended up back at his place because Joyce had misplaced her key. (Police later found it inside her purse.) "She came up of her own free will," Garry volunteered to the officer who arrested him.

He would explain how he and Joyce were sitting at the kitchen table early in the morning on December 28, talking about New Year's as her boys, 4-year-old Bradley and 3-year-old Clinton lay on the couch. "It was kind of romantic," said Garry. As he remembered the moment, "it could have been said that we were close to the act of making love."

But suddenly, he "snapped," as though he had been hit by a bolt of lightening. They ended up on the floor. He thought about having sex with her. Joyce was struggling and he was choking her, but somehow he managed to remove both their pants. He tried to have sex with her, but couldn't. The next thing he recalled was sitting on top of the woman he supposedly loved with his hand down her throat. Joyce was unable to breathe—she died from asphyxiation.

During the struggle, Bradley awoke, and Garry told him to go back to sleep. He could not be certain the boy did.

Garry wiped his bloody hand across Joyce's face, crawled off her, and walked around the apartment in a daze.

His next memory is of six in the morning. He washed the blood from his hands and decided he needed to get rid of the evidence. Garry gathered up Joyce's clothes and put them in bags in his stationwagon. He planned to take the clothes and Joyce to a downtown garbage dumpster. He dragged the body out of the kitchen and into the hallway at the top of the apartment stairs. But he quickly discovered he could not carry her down the stairs, and he couldn't stand the thought of her body thumping all the way down. Garry dragged Joyce back into the kitchen, then he went in the bedroom and fell asleep.

Garry awoke about four hours later. Joyce was still on the kitchen floor, and her boys were on the couch. Garry wasn't sure if they were asleep or not. He dragged their mother's body into the bedroom and locked the door.

"Something happened in the bedroom," he would later tell police. The pathologist found an empty beer bottle inside Joyce's body. Inserted after death, it had perforated the vaginal wall and was partly in her abdomen.

The best he could do by way of an explanation for that final indignity was to tell police: "I believed or I truly thought that she used her sexual capacity to benefit herself."

After exiting the bedroom, Garry had a new plan. He needed to get "rid" of Joyce's sons. He drove the youngsters out of the city, and abandoned them near the field where they were found. The boys were afraid and didn't want to get out of the car, so Garry removed them himself. Before driving away, Garry kicked Bradley several times in the face. He had learned from Joyce that the 4-year-old didn't like Garry. And Garry so needed to be liked.

On the drive back into the city, he revised his plan. He was going to try again to get Joyce's body to a dumpster. Instead, he drove to his parents' place and waited for police.

His statement to police was dated December 29, 1990, a day after the Mounties found Joyce's body. Garry was being questioned by RCMP Constable Brian Jarvis. He had read Garry's letters. As the prisoner grew more agitated, Jarvis suggested, if there was anything Garry wanted to ask, perhaps it would be easier if he wrote it out.

On a single foolscap sheet, Garry asked his question: "How are the Espedal children?" Jarvis told him the boys had been found the previous day and were in the hospital. Garry seemed relieved to hear their lives were no longer in danger.

When Garry was arrested, he had told the officers about Joyce. But he had not mentioned her boys. They were in the bitter cold for at least an hour and possibly as long as two hours before passers-by found them. Initially, police didn't realize the connection between the murder and the child abandonment.

Garry Ganton was sentenced to fourteen years in prison for the attempted murder of Bradley and Clinton Espedal. It will be served at the same time as the life sentence he received for the first-degree murder of their mother.

TRAIN NUMBER SIX

Freshly shaved, his hair neatly trimmed, John Woltucky slipped into his brand new dark pinstriped suit. He topped it off with a brownish-grey herringbone tweed overcoat and a stylish grey fedora hat. The dapper-looking, dark-haired, 25-year-old left an impression on the clerk at Saskatoon's Ritz Hotel where John had spent the night before boarding the train the next day.

A pair of brown Oxfords completed his travelling outfit. Those shoes, custom made, would surely take him places.

Anna Juswiak was also carefully choosing her clothes that Saturday. Admittedly, her choices were limited, but she had enough belongings to fill a couple of suitcases for her journey to Glenavon. Displaced by war, Anna had been in this country less than two years. She didn't have any relatives here or even close friends—until she met Stanley.

They had both come from the old country, sharing their Polish heritage. Stanley Kisilowski started working on the same Codette-area farm as Anna in April, and within a month they were a couple. A year had passed since then. Now she was in Saskatoon working for another family. Stanley was still in Codette. Weeks earlier, her future had seemed so uncertain, but it became clearer with Stanley's letter. He had made arrangements for the 23-year-old to temporarily stay with friends.

When her train arrived in Glenavon, she was to go to the hotel for the night and call the friends the next day. And Stanley reminded her not to spend money on anything for the baby. They could buy what they needed when they were together.

The baby—clearly unplanned, but now seemingly welcome, if Stanley's letter was any indication—would arrive in the fall. Stanley's one-year contract as a farm labourer would be fulfilled at the end of April. Then he would collect his salary and his bride-to-be from his friends' farm.

Anna didn't know Stanley's friends the Syndrowskis. She sent off a letter and received a telegram that bolstered her confidence: "Come to Glenavon as soon as possible. You are welcome at our home." It was dated May 1, 1950.

That was the day Stanley's friend Klem Syndrowski had understood Anna would actually arrive in Glenavon. He waited at the CPR station, but Anna didn't get off the train. Unsure exactly when she might get there, Syndrowski asked the storekeeper to meet the train again in a couple days, and then he sent off the telegram to Anna.

Four days later, she donned her green coat and wine-coloured hat and went to the train station. Her employer paid out $45 in wages, helped her buy an $8 train ticket and checked two suitcases and a parcel. Anna carried one inexpensive, brown suitcase with her as she boarded the train in Saskatoon.

Mary Pearson and a friend boarded Train Number Six in Regina that same Saturday. They were heading back home to Kipling after a shopping trip. Mrs. Pearson had bought a wine-coloured coat, and wondered about matching it with green shoes. She had ultimately settled on red. But she was struck by Anna's green coat and wine hat as the young woman and the gentleman with whom she had been sitting at the far end of the coach car walked past to get off at Glenavon shortly before 10 p.m.

A strong northwesterly wind was bringing in a spring snowstorm. The wind would howl through the night.

William Bruce was getting oats for his horses the next morning when he spotted Anna. Her green coat and blue skirt were hiked up around her waist. Her little wine hat lay nearby in the mud. Covered partly by a snow drift, Anna lay on her back between the Bruce's wind-weathered stable and the out-house, only three blocks from the CNR station—and in the same direction as the hotel. Her suitcase was nearby.

Anna had tried to fend off her attacker—if the green button ripped from the middle of her coat and the hair comb smashed to pieces beneath her body were any indication. The remainder of the broken comb held her dark hair, caked with mud and matted by blood, in place. Just four-foot-ten, she was no match for a man armed with a hammer. Anna had died almost instantly from five blows that smashed her skull. In death, her arms cradled her pregnant abdomen.

The stranger arrived wet and tired at the hotel in Kipling early that morning. The night clerk didn't have a room to offer; the hotel was filled with workers installing a pipeline. But there might be a room in about an hour when someone checked out, the clerk told him. At 6 a.m., in a nearly indecipherable scrawl, Les Beaudry from Portage La Prairie signed for room 3A and paid $2 up front.

He was still there that evening when two Mounties found him. The tweed coat was hung up on the door. Rifling through the man's suitcase, officers found a cheque book and a pay envelope marked "John Woltucky." It had held $12.47, his earnings as a prisoner collected upon his release one day earlier. The prison had bought his $13.85 ticket from Prince Albert to North Brandon. Asked for identification, the Canadian-born Woltucky, son of Ukrainian immigrants, produced his army discharge certificate. He had chosen to use a false name rather than be pegged as a convict.

His new stylish pinstripe suit, hat and overcoat were standard issue, given to all inmates upon their release—as if a new suit might be enough to make a new man. The Mounties noticed strips of gauze bandage, stained with blood, scattered

John Woltucky, 1950.

on the floor next to the Oxfords. He had been measured for the newly-made shoes in preparation for his release on May 4, but the footwear was still too tight.

And now John himself was in an equally tight spot.

He had a one-way ticket to Winnipeg—bought earlier in the day with a $20 bill—and an explanation for the $9 in coins jingling in his pocket and the $30 in his wallet. John had a reputation as a pretty good poker and bridge player at the prison. He had won the coins, he explained. The rest came from odd jobs picked up after his release.

The officers might have asked a few more questions, but at that moment a phone call was waiting for them in the hotel office.

John didn't wait. He had a train to catch. He was at the station, ten minutes away from boarding Train Number Six when he was arrested that night. As John emptied his pockets, the officers noticed a bank book in his suit coat. Anna had opened her account in January after taking the job in Saskatoon. She had deposited her life savings, $280.

What the officers did not find was Anna's purse, or the hammer John had retrieved from his personal effects before leaving prison.

The purse, black with a shoulder strap, had been bought for Anna by her employer's wife back in Codette. She easily recognized her gift at Woltucky's trial. Some boys shooting gophers on Mother's Day had found it in the mud along the tracks by Dalzell—between Glenavon where Anna had gotten off the train and Kipling where John had arrived at the hotel with his badly blistered feet.

They also found two tubes of lipstick. The red Max Factor matched the smear on the collar of Woltucky's brown and white striped shirt. Near the lipsticks and a ladies' hair curler was a photo of Anna, three baggage claims and a telegram. Although weathered and ripped, it still carried Syndrowski's welcoming message.

If John had been intent on raping Anna that night, it would seem he failed. There were no signs of a sexual assault. Rather, his desire seemed to have more to do with the few dollars she carried in her purse.

Or maybe, it wasn't really about that either.

John's mother recalled how after he returned from the war, her son always seemed nervous and jumpy. He was 16 when he enlisted in the army, lying that he was three years older. He would remain overseas for the next five years. When he came home, John often yelled out in his sleep: "They are coming." He didn't like to talk about that time, and his mother stopped asking.

When he landed in prison in 1949, he was convinced his fellow inmates were poisoning his food with a dark brownish substance resembling black pepper. It was retaliation, he believed, because he had informed against the other prisoners on a trivial disciplinary matter. He told doctors about the poisoning after he was transferred from the jail to the mental hospital. The poison gave him headaches, made his stomach burn, and interfered with his thoughts. Some of the psychia-

Yard site where the body of John Woltucky's victim was found, 1950. Copyright Department of Justice. Reproduced with the permission of the Minister of Public Works and Government Services Canada (2008). Source: Library and Archives Canada/Department of Justice fonds, RG13, B-1, Vol. 1706, file cc 742, Part 3.

trists thought he might be faking his delusions. In any case, they felt certain he didn't belong in the hospital. John went back to the prison in November, and was sent out to the community in his new suit six months later.

After Anna died, John spoke to the doctors again. He told them about the "radium machine" the Mounties were using in the walls of his cell to read his thoughts and make him say and do things. At the end of one interview, John let loose a hearty laugh without any apparent reason. "Oh somebody put a thought into my mind, I guess," he told the doctor.

After a dozen electric shock treatments John received at the Weyburn Mental Hospital, doctors were confident his delusions were still present, but no longer controlling his behaviour. He still believed the thought machine existed and could be used again, but the psychiatrists pronounced John fit to stand trial.

Twice Woltucky was found guilty and sentenced to die. (The appeal court overturned his conviction the first time.) Chief Justice James T. Brown called the case one of the most terrible he had presided over. "Any man who could have persisted in hammering the life out of this poor girl without justification or excuse for the sake of a few paltry dollars is a man whom we cannot have much pity for—he is a fiend in human form; and there is only one sentence that seems fitting for such a case," the judge said. He sentenced Woltucky to death.

"I may tell you now that I see very little chance of your escaping that penalty in view of the nature of this crime and the deliberate intent and premeditation with which it has been carried out," Brown added.

His prophecy proved false. That train never left the station. Woltucky's sentence was commuted to life.

TANGLED WEB

When he spotted the red 1998 Mercedes Benz, Anthony knew it would be perfect. It carried a hefty price tag, but the young entrepreneur didn't mind. He was rolling in so much dough, he often tossed the paltry $1 American bills into the garbage.

The cost of the sedan was $39,627.97.

No problem. No need for financing. Anthony was prepared to pay cash. That's when the business manager at the Regina dealership started to get a little nervous. After all, who knew where all that money came from?

Anthony tried to reassure him. He ran an online business, he explained. The websites were peddling pornography, but they were completely legal, he said. He had earlier told the salesman he sold nude photographs but stayed away from the "questionable material." Like Anthony himself, his customers often preferred to pay in cash.

Still, the dealership was a little reluctant to accept that amount of currency. Anthony was told he needed a bank draft. On his return the next day, he did have a draft, but only for $6,128. He paid the rest with cash. A lot of it was in $20 bills. To ease any further concerns at the dealership, he showed his Georgia driver's licence, and provided the names of his banks in Maryland, where he was born, and Georgia, where he had resided before moving to Regina three months earlier. The deal was sealed.

Anthony was so pleased with his purchase, he returned two weeks later to show the salesman the fancy new wheels and sound system he had added—for another $5,000 US. Anthony said he would probably be back in about a month's time, likely before the end of September 1999, to buy another vehicle.

The Mercedes was a gift for Anthony's girl.

They had met in the spring. The relationship was forged byte by byte. He was an American, living in a city known for its skyscrapers, lush canopy of trees, humid summers and beloved Georgia Bowl. She was in a Canadian city, where the winters were frigid, the tallest building was twenty-five stories, the predominant trees were elms not azaeleas, and football was played at Taylor Field. While they might have looked out different windows, they built a link between the two countries in cyberspace, meeting in Internet chat rooms; he at a computer in Atlanta and she at one in Regina. He was a computer graphics designer; she a computer programmer. The two clicked.

By May 1999, he and his computer had taken up residence in her Regina home.

It can be tough for any newcomer to get re-established in an unfamiliar city, but not for Anthony. Soon the money was rolling in—to three post office boxes in Regina, and one each in White City and Edmonton.

Most of his clients were U.S. college students. But the business also attracted an accused killer and a few customers from overseas. While they came from a variety of backgrounds, they were united in their desire for the products Anthony was selling. Like his girlfriend, they had connected with Anthony online.

For slightly less than a hundred bucks, they could be anyone they wanted to be. The college kids trying to get into the bar simply wanted to be 21. No one could be sure about the motives of the man who wanted to be five other people, or those from the Middle East who wanted to appear to be in the American military.

At *www.fake-id*, *www.id-s*, or *www.college-degrees*, they found what they sought: top-quality, "authentic" fake identification. For a mere $40, they could get a social insurance number; $75 bought a u.s. military card; a birth certificate was a deal at $79; while the price of a driver's licence varied, like $65 for Iowa or $95 for New York State, which required more ink. The websites offered college degrees, complete with signatures and watermarks, from more than two thousand universities around the world.

As one site boasted: "You will be able to fool anyone."

In time, the advertising changed a bit to indicate the identification was intended as a "novelty item." One of the sites reminded customers, "our ids come with a sticker (very tiny) on the front. Now if you choose to peel it off after it arrives, that is entirely up to you, and you assume all responsibility."

Novelty or not, the demand for fake ids was very real. Anthony's mailboxes overflowed with customers responding to the ads on the four websites. Thirty or more orders were coming in daily. Before long, they would number in the thousands. Most of the envelopes were arriving from south of the forty-ninth parallel. By July 1999, Canada Customs began to wonder why.

Anthony didn't get the chance to buy that second vehicle. His computer business crashed when police shut him down two months later. Officers found 1,228 envelopes holding cash, cheques and money orders—and more were arriving daily. There was also $900 us stuffed into a safety deposit box at a Regina bank.

Officers spent hours opening the envelopes and tallying the money that had been earned while the business operated for six months. When Anthony opted to plead guilty to possession of property obtained by crime in January 2000, the total from opened envelopes was sitting at $84,644 us and $695 Cdn. Another 439 envelopes had yet to be counted. And that didn't include the money the cops would never see. With no other source of income, it was clear Anthony had been living off his ill-gotten gains since moving to this country.

He was not actually producing the fake identification, his lawyer explained. That seemed to be supported by the obvious absence of any equipment in his home capable of producing the identification. Anthony was only in the business of processing the applications, a practice he didn't think was illegal.

He was wrong.

The judge agreed with the Crown and defence that Anthony had already spent enough time in custody—nearly five months since his arrest—but that didn't completely repay his debt to society. The government demanded cash. All of it.

Anthony forfeited every dime seized from his online business—close to $150,000—as well as two computers, and the red Mercedes Benz, which was carrying some of his mail in the trunk when police seized it. Immigration authorities picked up the tab to send him back to the States.

Initially charged as "John Doe" then "Anthony Soriano," the 30-year-old, first-time offender was Anthony Wayne Wright by the time of his guilty plea. At least that was the name on his birth certificate. Soriano was the name on his fake ID.

THE SALESMEN

Peering into the barren darkness, Johnny spotted head-lights. He wasn't using any on the pick-up he was driving. This was their biggest load yet, and he was not about to risk losing everything. They had a lot of money tied up.

Besides, Johnny knew the way—the backroads and fields he had covered countless times, usually at night. But he was equally sure mistakes could happen. Did happen. You couldn't be too careful.

A while back, one of their customers had called.

"I smelled something a couple days last week," he told Johnny. Not only was the businessman a customer, but his warehouse made a good drop-off point. He told Johnny about the van parked suspiciously across the street. And then there was that guy—the one he didn't recognize—who came in try-ing to buy something. The stranger left empty-handed.

Calls like that put everyone—including Johnny's friend Brock—on edge, especially tonight.

"Listen, you be careful," Brock's girlfriend had warned him.

"Yes ma'am," Brock replied, like an obedient school boy instead of a grown man of 53.

"I mean it," she said. "I don't even like you doin' what you're doin.'"

"I know," replied Brock, "but I've got a lot invested in this run."

Before the trip, he and Johnny had been busy working the phones, getting orders for their "red potatoes," "white potatoes," or maybe some "rum-flavored candies." They reminded their customers that Christmas was coming.

As Johnny neared his destination that cold, December night, his cell phone rang.

"A couple of good movies on tonight," said Brock.

"Oh well then. Well, I guess I'll come over," Johnny replied.

Then Johnny spotted the lights—and he wondered.

"Everything's cool. It's just me if you see some lights," Brock reassured him with another call. But Johnny and his friend Lone Sky—following behind in Johnny's orange truck, the one he called "the pumpkin"—still weren't in the clear.

Johnny called Brock again. "I was going to call you," Brock said, "and I was going to say, 'Hey fella, you can run, but you can't hide.'"

"You're all right this way. I'm going to parallel you," he said, a few minutes later, letting Johnny know he would be on the adjacent road.

Their journey ended at an old farmyard, just south of Estevan. They had made it. The forty-ninth parallel was behind them.

Ahead, there was money to be made.

* * *

The loaded U-Haul pulled up to the warehouse after lunch time the next day. Brent was following in a blue Ford Crown Victoria. Many of the customers didn't actually know him as Brent—to them, he was Johnny Two Feathers, who had a sidekick he called Lone Sky, or sometimes "Runnin' Whiskey."

For that's exactly what they were doing.

The RCMP had been listening for months to the conversations between Robert Brock Perry, the carpet salesman, his good friend Brenton Geoffrey Dyer, formerly a car salesman whose Ford dealership had hit a rough patch into receivership, and their customers. They heard the code words—like "red potatoes" for rye and "white potatoes" for vodka and the obvious "rum candies." The cops also heard the two salesmen grumbling about customers who asked for specialty items, like the liqueur Tia Maria.

"These people always think you're a liquor board store, don't they?" said Brent.

Brock agreed. "I got a new one yesterday, and the guy was asking for Club Royal or Canadian Club."

The "smell" picked up by the businessman—he was right. The man who had come into his shop in search of cheap American booze was a plainclothes officer. As for the van that never seemed to move, it had a camera facing out the rear windows to videotape customers picking up their "bags of potatoes."

The camera was also rolling when Johnny and Lone Sky loaded up one hundred and fifty cases of liquor—nine hundred bottles—at a bar in Alexander, North Dakota, on December 12, 1994. And they were watching the next day when that load, transferred to the U-Haul from the "pumpkin" truck and Brock's half-ton, arrived at a Regina warehouse. That's when the Mounties moved in and shut down the illegal booze business. Until then, about two thousand bottles of u.s. liquor, some with Canadian names, had been moved and sold across the border. The sellers turned a profit of about $32,000, but the taxman was out roughly twice as much.

The list of exhibits at the trial read like the remnants of an office party: a cardboard box for Heaven Hill light rum, a case of Canada House rye, a case of Kamchatka vodka, and plenty of invoices from the Hard Ride Liquor Store south of the border.

Brock Perry took a run at giving an explanation. The smuggling business was Brent Dyer's, not his. Their discussions, captured by RCMP, about getting together almost $16,000 before the last big haul—that was Dyer's money. Perry was only holding it for him. In fact, Perry was angry to discover Dyer was using his truck that December night. That's what Perry said.

But then why were the accused bootleggers in such good spirits, laughing in those conversations?

"Rather than being outraged, it's quite clear that both parties were, if anything, jubilant," Justice William Matheson noted.

Although separated in age by thirteen years, Brent and Brock had been buddies for four decades. Brent was eager to help his good friend. He pleaded guilty before Brock's trial and tried to take the rap. Brent said he began in 1993 with just a few boxes. As he got bolder and realized the strong market for cheap U.S. booze, a few cases grew to truckloads. He wore a hat and dark sunglasses and used the name "John" in the early days. Someone noticed two feathers sticking out of his hat one day, and he became "Johnny Two Feathers." Dyer insisted it was all his operation, driven by the demise of his car dealership.

But the pair had a tough time explaining away those troublesome tapes.

The RCMP heard Brock asking Brent about being seen together two weeks before the big shipment. Brent reassured him; it was dark.

"Oh, we just have a little thing going between the two of us that when we were seen together, we were always up to something," Brock later testified at his trial.

"People might think you're smugglers," prosecutor Alan McIntyre shot back.

"That's your opinion," Perry replied.

Brock and Brent were pretty good salesmen, but the judge wasn't buying their story.

"One would not only have to be credulous, but exceptionally obtuse to conclude that the intercepted communications relied on by the Crown mean anything other than as suggested by the Crown," said Matheson. He convicted Perry of eight charges of conspiracy and smuggling under the Customs Act.

The night of the last big load, Brock had spoken to his girlfriend upon his return. "Everything went well," he had assured her.

But the woman was right to worry. "You of all people, you know what they can do to you," she had warned.

Indeed, he did. Brock had been sent to jail in 1989 for liquor smuggling. This time, his friend Brent would share his fate. Their customers also found that cheap booze came at a high price. While the salesmen bought themselves time behind bars, their customers paid with fines.

DORA AND THE DEVIL MAN

She didn't like him. Not from the moment she saw him. Everything had been good before he came along. They had a perfect home, a perfect family, and Dora Pedhorodetsky was a devoted wife and mother. Then he showed up and ruined everything.

It was the fall of 1939—September 21 to be exact—when Dora's sister Olga brought him over. His name was Harry, and he made his living as a fortune teller. Olga and Harry had been going together pretty steadily that whole summer, and when Olga brought Harry to her sister's farm a few miles west of Ituna that day, she announced that the two were planning to get married. Dora was stricken by the news. It wasn't merely the age difference—Olga was 18, Harry 45—or the fact that Harry was rumoured to have a wife back home in Europe. Dora just couldn't stand him. Couldn't stand the thought of him, couldn't stand the thought of what her own dear children would think when they learned about their aunt's wanton behaviour. William, just seven years old, and little Olga, younger still. How would that innocent five-year-old child be affected by the actions of her namesake?

Yes, there was something about Harry that disturbed Dora very deeply.

She told her husband John that she thought Harry was a Devil Man.

* * *

After that day in September, things got worse for Dora and her family. Dora was a deeply religious woman, traveling the six miles from their family farm to the Greek Catholic Church in Ituna for the service every Sunday without fail, and holding lengthy prayer sessions with her children every morning and night. But that was before.

After the Devil Man came to their house, Dora couldn't pray. She would try, eyes closed tight, her palms pressed hard together, but thoughts of the Devil Man would seep into her mind no matter how hard she tried. She couldn't sleep either, and would lie awake night after night worrying about what would happen now that the Devil Man had entered their lives. Dora cried often, usually for no reason at all. John noticed that his wife's baking, once so delicious, was hard and bland. Her home-baked bread wouldn't even rise anymore, and would stay flat and dense no matter what she did.

John knew something was happening to his wife, something bad. Once, she walked a half-mile home from her mother's house when it was already near midnight, and she had always been afraid of the dark. Once, John saw her walking out in the snow barefoot on a freezing January night. John noticed all of these things, but he didn't know what to do, so he didn't do anything at all.

On the morning of January 29, 1940, Dora couldn't take it anymore. She waited in the kitchen until John left the house and headed to the barn. With her husband gone, Dora picked up a straight razor, grabbed her son William, and dragged the sharp metal blade across the child's throat. As the boy fell to the floor in a pool of blood, Dora grabbed her daughter. The five-year-old struggled and screamed as her mother brought the razor to the child's small neck. The little girl's screams brought John running into the house.

John burst into the kitchen and wrestled the razor away from his wife, stopping Dora before she could inflict more serious injuries on Olga. It was too late for William, who already lay dead on the floor. John took his wife and daughter to his brother Alex's house nearby. John was standing outside crying when Alex opened the door.

"My wife killed a child," John told him.

While Olga was being treated for the cuts her mother had inflicted, Alex took John and Dora to the RCMP detachment in Ituna. Dora wept as they traveled into town.

"Why was I born to be the murderer of my child?" she asked.

The men didn't answer.

* * *

At a preliminary hearing in February 1940, a jury decided that Dora Pedhorodetsky was insane when she murdered her son, and she was committed to a mental hospital instead of a jail.

Examining Dora in North Battleford, Dr. G.F. Nelson found her "mentally ill, depressed, confused and with the idea that she was under some outside control." The psychiatrist found the woman had a low IQ and a pre-existing mental condition, which had worsened steadily in the months after she met Harry.

Dora had been in the hospital for eight years when Dr. Nelson decided she was "emotionally normal and able to instruct her counsel." Dora Pedhorodetsky would stand trial for the murder of her son.

Facing her mother from the witness stand in a Melville courtroom, Olga, now 14, recalled the horrible scene all those years earlier.

"She stood back of my brother and she cut his throat. He just fell down," the girl testified. "I was close to him. Then she grabbed me and started to cut my neck. I screamed and Dad came in and grabbed me away from my mother."

Olga said her mother had always treated her well before that day. Asked whether she still loved her mother, Olga replied: "Yes, I do."

A jury took two and a half hours to consider the case, and then acquitted Dora Pedhorodetsky on the basis that she was insane at the time of the crime. She was taken back to the hospital where she had already spent so many years.

There was certainly no doubt that Dora Pedhorodetsky had killed her child. She had even given a full confession to the RCMP on the day of her son's death, telling officers she wanted to kill her children to save them from the worry that plagued her.

"I got up at morning so I thought to myself, I should have killed my kids so that they will not have as much worries as I do...," she had said, in her broken English. "I did it. I took a razor, cut neck of my poor son and am wanting to cut my daughter's neck. It is all in case of worrying."

THE SCHOOL MASTER

More than a decade had passed, yet Tracy had no trouble finding her way back into the tunnels. Of course, gone was the scrap of cardboard that had covered the cement floor where she had once lain. But she could still point out the small room, the one she called the cubbyhole. As a police officer watched, Tracy reached out with her hand and pointed to the spot where candles had burned fourteen years earlier. To her surprise, she felt something familiar. Today was November 6, 1993. Yet Tracy still found traces of candle wax and burnt matches. It might have been coincidence. It seemed almost unbelievable that such remnants would survive. But as Tracy knew, some things don't change with time. Like the school years that come and go, they continue their endless cycle.

* * *

Tracy was 13 when Mr. Foster became her home-room teacher in Grade 7 at Riverside School in Prince Albert. The junior high school teacher had a sense of humour that was more fit for the locker room than his classroom. She remembered how he would call the girls—always the girls—up to get a pencil from his desk, followed by, "Get your hands out of my drawers." Or he would curl up his finger to summon a student. "Do you see how easy I made you come." And he would grin.

Sometimes, he called them "wenches," and ensured the most developed girls sat at the front. He had a way of brushing up against them, touching their arms, shoulders, legs and buttocks.

Tracy was in Grade 9 the first time something happened. "Go down to the art room at noon," Mr. Foster told her, saying he needed help. He was waiting at the bottom of the stairs and opened the door to the service tunnels. They ran beneath the school to provide access to the boiler room and utilities. Mr. Foster grabbed Tracy by the hand, pulled her inside and shut the door behind them. It was dark and hot as he led her around the corner to the cubbyhole.

The teacher instructed his student to get undressed.

Mr. Foster was used to giving orders, and expecting people to follow them. He had been in the militia since he was 14 years old; he had lied about his age because he needed to be 16 to enlist. Over two decades, he worked his way up to the rank of major and became the commanding officer for the regiment in Prince Albert. He even served as an aide-de-camp to three lieutenant governors; it helped him earn two long-service medals for exemplary conduct. He retired from the militia in 1977, the same year he received a Teacher of the Year award.

Tracy would not so readily comply with her teacher's orders on this day. She pulled away and he pulled her back, closing his grip on her hand until it hurt. She said "No" when he told her to remove her clothes. But he was a man used to getting his way. He forced off her clothes, then forced himself on the terrified 15-year-old.

She said 'No!' louder, but Mr. Foster put his hand over her mouth. When he finished, Mr. Foster said: "Next time, get undressed yourself."

Indeed, there were too many next times. Mr. Foster kept turtles in his classroom, and Tracy was supposed to come feed them at noon hour—only to end up down in the tunnels. Sometimes, Mr. Foster brought candles, as if for a romantic rendez-vous. Maybe that's what he thought those meetings were. He would insist that Tracy say she loved him, that this was an affair—not the rape of a child by a man more than twice her age.

"No one would believe you if you told," he repeatedly told Tracy. He said he knew people in high places; that he would fail her in class; that he would go after her sister. Once, Tracy tried to tell her foster mother that she didn't like going to Mr. Foster's classroom. But the elderly woman told Tracy he was a nice teacher, and she shouldn't cause trouble. And so Tracy followed Mr. Foster's orders—obeying the notes he left at her desk that said simply "noon."

It wasn't always in the tunnels. Other times he would pick her up after school. He said he was driving her home, but would instead take her out to the military range. Tracy's arguments didn't matter.

With the end of Grade 9, there was some hope Tracy could put Mr. Foster and the junior high school behind her. Then, on Canada Day, Tracy discovered she was pregnant.

* * *

Jane had always thought of herself as a geek, a nerd. She liked school and got straight A's and B's. Mr. Foster's interest in her felt like an affirmation that she was female, that she could be attractive. The extra attention and privileges from her Grade 9 English teacher turned to fondling. Then one day he offered to drive her home. Saying he had to make a stop at the military range, he pulled over on one of the side trails. He lifted off Jane's glasses and set them on the dash, then had sex with his top student in his car.

After Jane went to high school, they met rarely, and Jane thought the relationship was over. She had moved on. Then Mr. Foster spotted Jane one day with her armful of books and offered to drive her home. He had to stop by the school for just one thing, and didn't want to be seen with her. He told her to wait, and he would return. She thought about escape then, but he had insisted she leave her books in his car—and she worried about losing them.

On the drive, she talked about her boyfriend, and how she had become a Christian, trying to make it clear she wasn't interested anymore.

At the range, she began to cry. But Mr. Foster was oblivious as he spread a blanket beneath a tree. As she lay there, the tears spilled down Jane's cheeks.

"No," she whispered. When Mr. Foster was done with the 16-year-old, he told her, "Now look what you've made me do . . . Well we might as well go then."

Back in the vehicle, Jane asked if he had ever cared for her, ever loved her even a bit. He grunted in reply.

Jane had never felt so alone. The teenage girl pulled out her diary when she got home. "Today I was raped," she wrote.

About a week passed when she got a message at her high school to phone Mr. Foster. She felt like a trained dog, obeying his command. She dialed the number, thinking he must be calling to apologize. Rather, he wanted to use her again—to slip a note under the door of two teachers he suspected of having an affair.

Jane asked to meet with them and then revealed Mr. Foster's accusation. Jane explained why Mr. Foster thought he could make such a demand of her. She told the two teachers about the sexual relationship she'd had with Mr. Foster throughout Grade 9 and about the recent rape.

But her teachers were more concerned about explaining that they weren't having an affair.

Three days after the attack, Jane went to a doctor, hoping she could provide some help. The physician did not believe the teen could have been raped by a teacher.

Jane never saw Mr. Foster again until she returned to Riverside years later as a substitute teacher herself. The stress of seeing him in the staff room each day finally drove her to go to a sexual assault centre, where a worker suggested she call police. She was convinced she wasn't the only victim. But Jane's efforts at reporting Mr. Foster to police failed to spark an investigation. The allegation was dated, and Jane the only complainant. She asked police to contact her if anyone else ever came forward.

Sixteen years after her rape, that day arrived.

* * *

Jennifer's love of animals took her to Mr. Foster's classroom where she could feed the turtles. When she was younger, she used to follow her older sister Trina up there—in defiance of their mother, who told them to stay away. All the children loved to see the turtles in Mr. Foster's room.

One day over the lunch hour, nine-year-old Jennifer was in to visit the turtles when she saw two other girls doing papier-mâché in the classroom. Jennifer joined them. Afterwards, while putting away the art supplies in an adjacent room, Mr. Foster, kneeling on the floor, asked Jennifer for a hug.

That's when he slipped his hands into her pants—just like he had done once before. Jennifer pushed him away and opened the door to return to the classroom. Another student guessed by the look on Jennifer's face that something wasn't right. She asked Jennifer if Mr. Foster had touched her. Then she asked if Jennifer wanted help to make it stop. Together, the two children went to the principal's office and told on Mr. Foster.

From the minute her daughters Trina and Jennifer had started at Riverside, their mother Tracy worried. But she couldn't tell her husband why she didn't want their children attending the school—not without revealing what had happened to her down in the tunnels, not without keeping the secret of how her eldest daughter had been conceived.

Even after Tracy had left high school with the birth of her daughter Trina, Mr. Foster continued to insinuate himself into her life. He stalked Tracy, describing her wedding despite not having been among the invited guests. He would appear at her workplace to talk about "the good times"—and how it could be good again. He insisted she accept his gifts, like the medallion he made for her daughter. It sat in a drawer for years until becoming trial evidence.

When Mr. Foster demanded to know if she had told anyone about him, Tracy replied, "I just want to forget about the past." But Mr. Foster didn't like rejection. Her children might find themselves in his classroom, or her husband Tom could find a bomb under his vehicle, he told her. She had little doubt he could do it with his military training. One day she found an envelope outside her home with a bullet and a stencilled note:"This is for Tom."

Fearing he would kill her husband, she agreed to meet her former teacher one Friday in 1988. He drove her out to the military range—and raped her once again. "This is never going to end," she thought. The threats continued—about revealing their "affair" to her husband or taking away Trina. Tracy couldn't bear anymore. She went to Riverside to tell Mr. Foster she was going to kill herself. The calls stopped. But she would still see him driving past her house.

It ended for good when Tracy was called to the school office about Jennifer. She recognized the frightened look on her child's face. "I'm not going to let Jennifer go through being haunted by him and harassed," she vowed. She told her husband what had happened to her when she was one of Mr. Foster's students. And more difficult yet, she told Trina, the daughter she had given birth to at Holy Family Hospital, about her biological father, Mr. Foster.

Then she told police.

When Tracy and Jennifer went forward with their complaints, so did Jane as well as Misty, a Grade 8 student also raped in the tunnels, lured there by the teen's fascination with the occult. Like Tracy a decade earlier, Misty used to go to Mr. Foster's classroom at lunch time to feed the turtles.

* * *

Dennis Winston Foster had been a teacher for thirty years; he retired once the allegations surfaced. He had three separate trials on charges involving nine former students. He was convicted of sexually assaulting four of them. The offences spanned sixteen of the nineteen years he taught at Riverside. Foster, then 54, was sentenced to six and a half years in prison after his first trial in 1994. He received no additional time after being convicted at his second trial. A psychologist at the prison asked Foster to estimate the number of sexual assaults in which he was involved. "One hundred and twenty, maybe," he replied.

A probation worker preparing a pre-sentence report in 1999 after the second trial stated:"It is this writer's opinion that Mr. Foster has yet to become honest with himself regarding the actual number of victims he has."

Throughout the trials, while he was behind bars, and after he was out, the man who ensured some students never felt safe at school continued to collect his teacher's pension. A portion of that money was spent on child support for the daughter he fathered with his student. The teacher used to giving orders was directed to keep paying until the young woman received a university education.

* Tracy, Jane, Trina, Jennifer and Tom are pseudonyms. A court order prohibits publication of any information that would identify them.

PUBLIC TRUST

John T. Nicolle, a young, unemployed bookkeeper, left his apartment in Regina on the evening of August 17, 1939, for an important appointment at the Hotel Saskatchewan. Nicolle was to meet with two men, A.H. White and Dr. C.G. Cox, both respected veterans of the Great War, and now trustees of a charitable fund that provided money to struggling veterans. White also ran the Western School Supply Company, where Nicolle had worked until a year earlier.

As Nicolle's wife, Barbara, would later recall, Nicolle went out that night planning "to discuss getting back his job over a bottle of liquor."

Nicolle certainly liked his liquor, and therefore Barbara wasn't overly surprised when he didn't return home that evening. But when her husband still hadn't come home three days later, Barbara began to get concerned. Nicolle had once told Barbara that if he were to disappear under mysterious circumstances, she should look for a letter hidden inside their home, and so, recalling his instructions, she soon began scouring the apartment for a message.

Two weeks later, she finally found the note. It had been penned by Nicolle the previous fall, and it read:

"Dear Barbara;

This is to advise you that, in view of the negotiations I have had with A. H. White, regarding his embezzlement of funds from the Saskatchewan Canteen Fund, I am and have been fearful for some time for my life.

You understand from what I have told you from time to time that I have full proof of his activities and he is afraid I might squawk, and for this reason, if perchance I should meet an untimely end or leave this life under suspicious circumstances you will be in a position to advise the authorities.

I might add that both lower drawers of your vanity dresser have false bottoms, and therein you will find all evidence.

Best of love and luck to both you and Junior."

It was signed, "Your loving husband, John T. Nicolle"

Barbara Nicolle called the police.

* * *

The Saskatchewan Canteen Fund was made up of profits from canteens operated in England and France during the First World War, a surplus built with the dimes and quarters of men who had enlisted to serve their countries in the Great War, and relied on the canteens for everything outside their usual army rations.

At the war's end in 1918, Canada's canteen profits were well over $2,000,000, and Saskatchewan's share came to nearly $176,000. As in the rest of the country, the money was eventually turned over to a board of appointed trustees so it could be given to veterans who were in need of help.

In Saskatchewan, the trustees appointed to manage the Canteen Fund were White, Cox, and, after an earlier trustee retired, Colonel A.G. Styles. All of these men were veterans who had themselves served overseas, and were highly trusted and respected in the province.

Working under the Canteen Funds Act of 1925, the men would administer all the money in the fund, including processing grant and loan requests by veterans, a task that became especially demanding as the Depression settled hard into the province in the 1930s.

John Nicolle was working for White at the Western School Supply Company in the mid-30s, when he began to question White's management of the charitable fund. Nicolle found torn papers in his boss's wastepaper basket, which Nicolle would then take home and paste back together on fresh sheets of paper. The letters contained clear evidence of fraud and embezzlement from the fund by White and his fellow trustee, Cox. Nicolle soon collected seventeen such letters, which he secreted under a false bottom in his wife's dresser drawer.

But instead of taking his suspicions to the police, Nicolle had gone to Cox and White. The three men had then worked out an arrangement, and it was through that arrangement that Nicolle had been able to maintain his comfortable lifestyle, despite the fact he had not worked in more than a year.

For Nicolle, it seemed blackmail was just as lucrative as bookkeeping—but it was also more dangerous. Nicolle had told his wife on a few occasions that he feared for his life.

Around the same time, the Canteen Fund's secretary, Ruby Kirkby, was also starting to have concerns about the way the money was being administered. The keen-eyed secretary had noticed missing paperwork and odd-looking signatures, but every time she tried to mention her concerns to White, he brushed her aside. Kirkby grew even more uneasy in the first days of September 1939, while chatting with a friend about the Second World War. Kirkby had been wondering whether any of the Canteen Fund trustees would be called up for service, when her friend said something unexpected.

"This person said White and Cox wouldn't be called up as they were going to the penitentiary for 10 years for stealing from the Canteen Fund, as they had been issuing cheques in fictitious names and cashing them," she would recall later.

When she told White what her friend had said, White laughed it off.

But others, including the police, did not find the matter quite so humourous. After examining the documents found at the Nicolles' apartment, and with Nicolle still missing, police had been taking a very close look at the activities of Cox and White. It was a difficult and complex investigation, hampered further by the fact that Ruby Kirkby had destroyed nearly all of the canteen fund documents on earlier orders from White. Working through the files alphabetically, Kirkby had incinerated everything up to the letters 'So-' by the time she was approached by police.

Still, even with only the last part of the alphabet to work with, the case against White and Cox was significant.

There was ample evidence that Cox and White had colluded to issue cheques to people who had not applied for them, people who were not entitled to them, people who were dead, and, sometimes, people who had never existed in the first place. Since all Canteen Fund cheques required two signatures, Cox and White would sign for one another. The men then forged signatures or used their friendly relationships with unwitting businesses like Regina's Novia Café to cash the cheques and keep the money.

"I never got a nickel from them," said David Hibbs, looking at three cheques purported to have been cashed by him.

R.J. Rogers was equally surprised to see his name signed on a cheque for $210.

"It's not my signature," he said.

The men were merely two among many. In all, $30,000 was directly proven to have been stolen from the fund over several years, though the total amount of the fraud was actually believed to be closer to $40,000.

As police continued their investigation in the fall of 1939, Ruby Kirkby demanded a meeting with Cox and White in Saskatoon. Though Cox originally put her off, Kirkby was insistent, and the two struck a plan to meet at the LaSalle Hotel on October 24. Cox never showed up. Instead, he was found just outside Saskatoon that same day, dead from a single gunshot wound. The shell was fired from his own shotgun, but it would later be ruled an accident.

Within weeks, White was charged with theft for the missing Canteen Fund money, but the charge was not immediately served because White was ill and bedridden at his home in Regina. He committed suicide by drinking poison on December 26, before he could face the charge.

With Cox and White dead, a public inquiry was called to look into the shocking fraud committed by two so highly trusted gentlemen.

"As so often happens, they in whom one has the most implicit confidence can the most easily deceive, if they set out to do so," Justice Donald Maclean wrote at the inquiry's conclusion in 1940.

Despite a search around the continent, John T. Nicolle was never seen or heard from again.

HOSTAGE

Notebook poised, pen in hand, reporter Al Rosseker stood at the ready. The five Regina police officers were also prepared; one had a shotgun poised and at the ready. Standing together in the hallway of a Regina rooming house, the crime reporter and the cops had come for the same person—a man Al knew only as "Ray."

Ray had told the police he wanted to talk to a news reporter. Al had a standing offer with his city editor at the *Regina Leader-Post* that he was ready to chase the big scoops. He was hunched down near one of the police cruisers so he could keep an ear to the police radio when Constable Dave Quick approached and asked if Al was willing to speak to Ray. It was some time later when the reporter reflected on the last radio transmission he had heard before walking into that rooming house. The radio had crackled with word that Ray was threatening to shoot if anything moved on the street.

Ray was armed with a .303-calibre rifle carrying nine rounds of ammunition, and he already had one hostage.

As far as Ray was concerned, he didn't actually have the right hostage—not the one he was really after when he went to the office of the Unemployment Insurance Commission that afternoon on February 8, 1973. He had asked to see the district manager, Ivan Lake, when he arrived shortly after 2 p.m., but Ray was directed to another official. When he left,

Ray told the staff he'd be back in ten minutes—and he was a man of his word. On his return, the 21-year-old, dressed in a navy parka, was toting his rifle.

Ray randomly grabbed Fergie Foster and pointed his gun at the man's back. "Okay everybody. I want to see Mr. Lake right away or this guy is going to get it right here," Ray shouted.

Lake opened his office door to see what the ruckus was, spotted Ray and his gun, and quickly closed the door again. Ray waited for a few moments. "It's no use," he proclaimed before directing Foster toward the door.

Foster was like Ray—looking to UIC for assistance to help him out between jobs. Foster's sister was waiting outside in the car when she saw her brother exit with a gun pointed at his head.

"You shut up, or I'll shoot him for sure," Ray snarled in frustration. Ray held the back of Foster's coat with one hand, and pointed the gun with the other. He made his 30-year-old hostage walk in front of him at gunpoint for three blocks as a crowd of police officers and spectators followed. The tense, forced march ended at Ray's home, a three-storey rooming house at 2136 Smith Street. Ray made Foster open the door and walk up the stairs to Ray's third-floor suite. At gunpoint, Foster barricaded the door with a dresser. Ray put a table in front of the window. He told his captive not to try anything or he would shoot him in the shoulder.

About a dozen police officers, some armed with shotguns, had the house surrounded. But alas, it was not the cops Ray wanted to see, but a reporter. In Ray's eyes, at this moment the pen was truly mightier than the sword. The cops wanted to lock him up; a reporter could release Ray's words.

Constable Quick grabbed Al and told him to stick close as they went in the back entrance of the house. The man with the badge acted as a human shield, keeping his body in front of the man with the pen just in case the man with the gun changed his mind.

Al stood on the landing leading to the third floor. This would be a long-distance interview, the questions and answers shouted through a firmly closed door. Al spent the next five minutes discussing Ray's problems.

Ray felt no different than the hostage he held. He too was a man with a gun to his head. Ray had been without work since November; his UIC cheques had stopped coming in January; he was behind in rent; and his wife had been forced to return to her family in Ontario. He needed his UIC benefits, but the money was not forthcoming. He had been to the UIC office three times the week before. Al assured him his story would be carried by the media, then the reporter headed back down the stairs while Superintendent Dennis Chisholm and Inspector Norm Doane continued talking to Ray.

Ray wanted to exchange one hostage for another—Foster for the UIC's Lake. The officers refused that request, but Lake was allowed to speak to Ray and promised to look into his claim for benefits.

At some point, the hostage-taker named his price—not millions or thousands. Ray wanted exactly $268. It was the total of two $134 cheques he believed UIC owed him.

The police quickly got together the money. Doane slid the bills under the door. On Ray's orders, the veteran cop then backed off, down the stairs. A commotion broke the stalemate seconds later, as someone exited the room. It was the hostage, and he was $100 richer. Ray had paid the otherwise unemployed man for his two hours of trouble.

Al interviewed Ray a second time. The holed-up man said he didn't want the media attention for himself, but he wanted to publicize the problems with UIC, as he saw them. "There was just too much buck-passing at that place," he said. Unfortunately, none of those bucks were coming his way. He had been scraping together money from friends for six weeks to get by, he told the reporter. Desperate and destitute, Ray had phoned the welfare department that morning to see if anyone there could help. He was told he did not qualify for welfare—because he was eligible for UIC. Only he had not been getting his UIC. That was the problem. And Ray believed he wasn't the only captive of bureaucracy. He wanted the country and the world to know. He wanted to hear his story on the radio.

Al and Chisholm spoke to Harold Hamilton, sitting in the CKCK radio newsroom. Hamilton had Ray's story on the air for six that evening. By putting a transistor radio in the hallway, the police made sure Ray, who was sounding suicidal, heard it.

Al talked to Ray again shortly after the broadcast.

"The time I'm gonna spend in prison is just a small contribution to all the other persons who are constantly being shoved around by the UIC office," he told the reporter.

Ray came walking down the stairs with Chisholm shortly after six o'clock. Three hours had passed since he had walked into the UIC building with his gun. Ray had said his piece, and now he was ready to surrender peacefully.

The reporter and the prisoner rode together to the police station in the police cruiser. Ray told Al he hoped others might try to fight the system—although he was not recommending the means he had used. He said he really didn't want to hurt anybody.

Philip Raymond Bourget pleaded guilty to kidnapping and was sentenced to fifteen months in jail. Prosecutor Arnold Piragoff had asked for a much stiffer penalty, lest other people think they could take similar actions—against welfare officials, ministers of the Crown, or even judges. "That's why I have an officer sitting there," Judge Lloyd Hipperson replied.

The judge seemed more persuaded by the words of Bourget's lawyer George Tkach. "He never got any humane treatment at all. I would ask for a little from the court," the lawyer pleaded.

As Hipperson imposed the sentence, he wondered if the "whole sorry business" might have been avoided by a long-distance call—over a telephone line, not through a door.

Bourget's benefits had been interrupted while his claim was investigated. Unemployment Insurance ultimately authorized payment of the $268 Ray was due before his drastic actions. But the payment had to come from the UIC office in Winnipeg. Ray was held hostage by Canada's postal service.

His cheque was in the mail.

BITTER PORRIDGE

Carefully unwrapping the paper off a flower-patterned saucer, the coroner held it out to the man with the pigtail, thin black moustache and a wisp of a beard. Mack Sing solemnly grasped the saucer and fell to his knees. On his second attempt, he managed to shatter the china plate.

"Your soul will be cracked the same as the saucer if you swerve from the truth," the interpreter assured Sing. Still on his knees, Sing nodded gravely in response, agreeing to tell all he knew about the events leading up to the death of John Fortune.

* * *

A 20-something labourer, Fortune had been one of the boarders gathered around the breakfast table early Thursday morning at William Steele's place. The restaurant-owner dished out bowls of porridge, followed by a more substantial second course. But most of the plates came back to the kitchen with the ham and eggs largely untouched. Mrs. Steele assumed the men were running late for work and took advantage of the unexpected break to squeeze in her own breakfast. She helped herself to a bowl of porridge and filled one for her husband. He hadn't even tasted it when a stableman came running in to ask if there was any porridge left.

He wasn't looking for seconds.

"For God's sake, don't give them anymore," Joe shouted. "All the men who have eaten it are sick."

The men who moments earlier had been dining at Steele's Capital Restaurant in Regina on August 8, 1907, were now doubled over in pain in the nearby stable. All of them were vomiting. By the time Steele arrived, those stricken the worst were stretched out on the floor. Before he was overcome, boarder Rory Campbell, a machinist, had made it as far as the J. I. Case Company warehouse where he worked.

They blamed Steele's porridge for their sudden illness.

Nine men were sick. Mrs. Steele was also mildly ill, but not like the men who had polished off their bowls of porridge. Four men ended up at the Victoria Hospital. That's where John Fortune died that evening.

By suppertime, Mack Sing from the neighbouring restaurant was in custody and the hunt was on for its proprietor Charlie Mack.

Also known as Fook, Sing had come to Canada from China a decade earlier as a 10-year-old boy. While that name appeared alongside Charlie's on the one-year lease for the B.C. Restaurant, Sing/Fook denied having signed it. The accused man swore he was not Charlie's business partner but his servant, working as a waiter and cook.

He said Charlie was in charge of buying the food and making the porridge. A day before the men fell ill, Sing went to the Capital on Charlie's orders to borrow some rolled oats, he told the inquest through an interpreter. Steele had obliged, pouring the oatmeal from a sack into a one-gallon can Sing had brought with him. Sing returned that same evening with a full tin to repay the favour. Steele watched as the oatmeal was poured into the sack.

The two talked business.

In response to a question from Sing, Steele said he had seventeen boarders at the Capital. The B.C. Restaurant had only five.

"You do good business. I do no business," said Sing in his broken English. "I soon go Winnipeg," he added.

Charlie Mack had opened his restaurant on Lorne Street that April. Three months later, Steele started up the Capital just a few feet away. Before long the new restaurateur had poached many of Charlie's customers. Police suspected there was more than porridge simmering in the B.C.'s kitchen.

Dr. George Charlton, provincial bacteriologist, tested the porridge at his lab, where he mixed it with two other chemicals and applied heat. The resulting gas left a silvery-black film on a piece of cold porcelain—a tell-tale sign the porridge was laced with arsenic.

"Oatmeal is probably the best material to put arsenic into. This poison has a metallic taste, rather disagreeable if taken alone. There is a slight bitterness about oatmeal, just enough to disguise the peculiar taste of arsenic," he suggested. The porridge contained so much poison that even a tablespoon was enough to make anyone sick.

A week after Fortune died, Cyrus Winters, another boarder who had dined on the porridge, also passed away.

The police had plenty of questions for Charlie Mack—but no one had seen him since the morning the men at the rival restaurant fell ill.

The Royal North West Mounted Police issued instructions to detain any Chinese man resembling Charlie. One man was pulled off an eastbound train passing through Qu'Appelle and hauled back to Regina. Turned out he was a well-known laundryman headed to Indian Head to visit his brother.

Intent on getting their man, four officers, with the help of an interpreter, raided the Chinese quarter on Osler Street beginning late August 23 and extending into the early morning of August 24. By 4 a.m. every known Chinese man in Regina, some of whom had been peacefully asleep when police came calling, had been taken by bus to city hall. Each of the sixty-seven detainees was in turn questioned about his name, occupation and residence. The officers opened trap doors, turned cellars upside down, and searched through cupboards and under beds—to no avail.

"Charlie Mack is still missing, but the police now feel confident that he is not hidden anywhere in Regina," read that day's *Morning Leader*.

Four days later, the newspaper carried a story about charges—but not against Charlie Mack.

Corporal C.H. Hogg of the RNWMP, Chief Reuben James Harwood of the city police, and two other local constables had received summonses to appear in court. The officers were accused of unlawfully detaining four of the Chinese men picked up in the raid. It was a private prosecution launched by a local lawyer hired by the men.

While the police officers were all freed on their own recognizance, having never actually been arrested, Sing remained in jail awaiting his trial for the murder of John Fortune.

Sing was back on the witness stand that November. He told the court he was Catholic and quite willing to swear on the Bible, but prosecutor Alex Ross didn't want to take any chances. In addition to taking his oath in the usual manner by kissing the Bible, Sing also wrote his name on a piece of paper that was set aflame in the courtroom.

"If you don't tell the truth, your soul shall be consumed as that piece of paper," the clerk told him. Then Sing repeated the same story he had told at the inquest about knowing nothing of the toxic porridge eaten by the men at the Capital. His soul was spared. The jury took only half an hour to reach a verdict. The men found him not guilty.

Charlie was never found.

The police officers charged in the raid also walked on the criminal charges. The Crown decided there was insufficient evidence to prosecute them. But unlike the man they sought that night for a double murder, the officers didn't completely escape. They were successfully sued for false arrest and imprisonment by several of the men they had detained. The judge called the actions of the experienced officers "altogether irregular and illegal" and awarded $25 in damages.

LIPSTICK KISSES

It wasn't the most romantic place to start a relationship. Angie met Cliff at the Riverbend Institution, a minimum security prison in Prince Albert where Angie was working part time as a hairdresser. The warden introduced them in December 1998, on Angie's first day of work. Cliff was assigned to be her guard, staying with her while she worked, and making sure none of the prisoners did anything to scare or hurt her. Angie didn't even know Cliff was an inmate at first, and by the time she found out he was serving a seven-year sentence for sexual assault, she had already started to like him.

The 34-year-old single mom hadn't always had the best luck with men, but she and Cliff hit it off right away. They had a lot in common, and Angie felt sorry for him. She was someone who liked to help people, and she knew he needed help. She wasn't scared of Cliff at all. She could tell that even the prison guards liked and trusted him, and she felt like she was in safe hands.

"He was a gentleman," she said. "He was a kind person."

When Angie asked to be put on Cliff's visitor list a short time later, she was told she couldn't work at the prison if she was going to pursue a personal relationship with one of the inmates. She liked Cliff enough that she didn't mind leaving the job, even though she needed the money.

In the months that followed, the relationship between the two continued to grow deeper, and when Cliff got day parole

Angie agreed to be his support person on the outside. She would stop by the Red River Roping and Riding Club where Cliff worked whenever she could, and they would talk on the phone and write letters every day. Before long, Angie was falling for him.

"Did I tell you about this beautiful person that's entered my life?" she wrote in a letter to Cliff early in 1999. "He's good-looking, great body, real cute bum, dancing eyes and a grin to die for. Oh, and he's a nice guy, too. What a package. The guy upstairs must have finally broken down and decided I was doing a good job because I don't know how else I could be granted such a gift, one I plan on treasuring for a long time."

Angie marked some of the letters with lipstick kisses. On others she drew little cartoons or hearts with their names inside. On the last day of February, Cliff got down on one knee and proposed. Angie accepted, saying she would be proud to walk down the aisle and become Mrs. Clifford Howdle. Cliff had been spending time with her two boys, and he and Angie started imagining a life together on a ranch in Alberta.

But, as sometimes happens, things started to cool.

It started at Cliff's parole hearing that spring, festering doubts and nagging questions that left Angie unsure about the future of their relationship. And he seemed so needy, too, always wanting so much of her time, more maybe than she wanted to give. Angie ended it on May 16, telling Cliff that their romance was over, though she promised to continue to help him as he adjusted to life outside prison.

. Despite his deep feelings for Angie, Cliff seemed to understand, and he told her he would rather have her as a friend than not at all. He even asked if she could still cut his hair for him the next morning on his way to work. Angie said she would.

Cliff showed up at Angie's Prince Albert trailer just before nine in the morning, not long after Angie's kids had left for school. He told Angie he needed to postpone the haircut because there was something wrong with his truck. The truck was running so badly it had barely made it to her trailer, he said, and he was worried it would break down on his way to work. Cliff asked Angie if he could borrow her car for the day, but Angie said she would give him a ride to work instead.

Cliff seemed happy and chipper as they sat together at Angie's kitchen table drinking coffee, even playfully asking her if they could make love. When Angie said no, he laughed it off.

"Well, you can't blame me for trying," he said.

Angie was driving Cliff to work when Cliff confided he was thinking of breaking his parole and going on the run. When he asked Angie to pull over so they could talk about it, she did, parking her car near a grove of trees on a quiet dirt road. With the car stopped, she pleaded with Cliff to reconsider, to think of his three beautiful children. She told him he could go away for a long time. As they talked, Cliff suddenly reached toward Angie and roughly grabbed a handful of her hair. His eyes went cold.

"You should have made love to me this morning, bitch," he said. "Because now I'm going to fuck you the way I want to."

He dragged her out of the car by the hair, pulling her violently over the console and gearshift and out the door. Then he pushed her down onto the hood of the car and told her to do what she was told. Angie had never heard his voice sound that way. He didn't even look like the person she had known; he had a look of violence she'd never seen in him before. Then he raped her.

Cliff bound Angie's hands with plastic ties and threw her on the ground, trying to tie her ankles as she kicked and struggled against him. Angie resolved that she would do whatever she could to make it through the day.

"This morning is not going to be the last time I see my kids," she vowed to herself.

Angie tried to reason with Cliff, telling him she wouldn't call the police, that he wouldn't be in trouble if he stopped. She was relieved when she finally convinced him to take her home, believing she might at least have a chance of survival. When they got back to Angie's trailer, Cliff had calmed down. Angie put on a pot of coffee, and the two sat together smoking, drinking coffee and talking, with Angie doing everything she could to diffuse the situation. After a couple of hours, it seemed she had finally convinced Cliff to go back to work. But when Cliff went to kiss Angie goodbye, he tried to rip off her clothes. He told Angie he wasn't going to rape her this time. He said this time they were going to make love.

Angie told Cliff she had to let the dog out first, but when she got to the door she didn't wait for the dog. She ran out of the house, yelling that she had been raped and that the rapist was still in her house.

As Angie ran next door to the trailer where her brother and sister-in-law lived, Cliff sat placidly at the kitchen table smoking. Then he walked out of the trailer, got into the truck, and drove slowly out of the yard. Angie was struck by how tranquil he was.

"He drove like he was going to a lunch date or a meeting or whatever else," she said.

And she noticed that his truck wasn't broken down at all.

* * *

Judy and Richard arrived back at their farm north of Prince Albert in the late afternoon after dropping off their grand-daughter in the city. They walked in the back door together and Judy was halfway through the kitchen when she turned around to say something to her husband. As she did, a man grabbed her roughly from behind and held a knife to her neck.

It was Clifford Howdle. He hit Richard on the head with a wooden cutting board, then tied him up and put duct tape across his mouth. Howdle raped the 55-year-old woman twice as her husband lay just feet away, desperately struggling to get free. When Richard broke his arms loose, Howdle hit him in the head with the cutting board and tied him up again, then continued his assault on Judy.

Howdle got Richard's straight razor and started shaving off his moustache and goatee as he paced back and forth in the house in front of his two victims. He took the couple's hunting rifle and shells, and then grabbed Richard, pulling the 65-year-old outside and shoving him into the trunk of the couple's car.

Howdle shoved Judy into the backseat. She noticed he was well equipped for whatever he had planned, with a duffel bag full of chocolate bars, doughnuts, drinks and apples. Howdle got into the driver's seat, pulled out of the yard and headed onto the highway.

As they drove, he promised Judy he would let the couple go when it was dark, and she desperately hoped he was telling the truth.

But as the sun fell on that long May day, Howdle told her he had changed his mind. He said she had not yet satisfied him.

It was a long night riding through desolate back roads and lonely highways, and as dawn broke Judy was growing increasingly worried about her husband. She hadn't heard anything from the back of the car since they left the house more than twelve hours earlier. Howdle had stopped once and looked in the trunk, hitting Richard with the butt of the gun before slamming the trunk shut once again.

By morning, Howdle was nearly out of gas. He had parked the car to wait for a service station to open when he pulled Judy outside and forced himself on her again. Then he shoved Judy into the trunk with her husband. It was dirty and dry in there, hard to breathe, but there was one thing for Judy to be happy about: Richard was alive.

Lying together in the dark, Judy and Richard felt the car rumble into the parking lot of a gas station, and heard the attendant chatting with Howdle.

"Be careful, don't pick up any hitchhikers. There's a parolee on the loose," the woman was saying.

"I don't pick up hitchhikers," Howdle assured her.

* * *

Lorraine's day started like any other. Her husband and son headed off to work at 7:45 that morning, and the girls—her daughter and her son's fiancée—left together about fifteen minutes later. With everyone gone, Lorraine poured herself a bowl of cereal and was talking on the phone with her mother when she heard a car pull into the yard.

Glancing outside, Lorraine saw a man walking toward the house. He was tall, probably over six feet, and heavy set with a tussle of curly brown hair. Lorraine thought the man looked normal enough and decided that he, like many of those who stopped at their farm, was probably lost. She was right. Meeting Lorraine at the door, the man asked for directions to a house in the area. But even though she knew the area well, Lorraine had never heard of the people he was asking about, and she said goodbye to her mother so the stranger could use the phone.

The man asked Lorraine if her husband might know the place he was looking for, but Lorraine said her husband wasn't home. He asked if her children would know.

"Well, the one is working and the other two are in school," she told him.

At that, Howdle dropped the phone on the floor, then grabbed Lorraine hard around the neck.

"You should never have let me know that you were here by yourself," he said.

The two struggled on the floor of the kitchen, with Lorraine fighting valiantly despite the fact that he was more than double the size of the petite, ninety-seven-pound woman.

When Howdle finally got control, he dragged Lorraine to the car by the hair. She screamed for help, but no one was around to hear.

Howdle stopped again on a back road outside town.

"Now I'm going to rape you," he told her. "Oh, you're going to love this."

When the violent assault was over, Howdle shoved Lorraine into the backseat, tied up her hands, then trussed them to her feet with a plastic cord. He tried to put duct tape on Lorraine's mouth but she managed to get the tape off, and he didn't bother putting it on again. He was getting tired. As they sat in the car, Howdle told Lorraine he was going to commit suicide.

"What good would that do?" she asked.

Howdle said he was going to shoot himself, and told Lorraine to finish him off if he didn't succeed with the first shot. Lorraine said she couldn't do that with her hands tied, and after thinking about that for a few minutes, Howdle cut off her ties.

"You know, you remind me of my girlfriend," he told her. "Just in some of the things you say."

He told Lorraine he had raped his girlfriend and a 55-year-old woman.

"I didn't want to hurt either one of them and if I commit suicide I won't hurt anybody else," he said.

Howdle got out of the car and opened the trunk. Judy and Richard cowered inside, and Howdle told them he was letting everybody go. He wrote a note to Angie on a cigarette package and passed it to Judy. The note said: "Dear Angie, you are and will always be the love of my life. Sorry. Love Cliff. None of this is your fault."

Clifford Howdle stood alone on the road with the loaded gun as Judy, Richard and Lorraine drove away. Judy backed the car at least half a mile from him before turning around. She didn't want to take her eyes off him.

RCMP officers found Howdle in the ditch a few minutes later. He said the gun jammed, so he'd decided not to kill himself.

At his trial, Howdle blamed his behaviour on a serious car accident several years earlier that had put him in a coma for nearly three weeks. He said he thought a brain injury, acne medication, and a feeling of rejection had put him in an altered state, leaving him unable to control his actions. He testified he thought all the women he raped were Angie, and believed that if he could just make love to them, it would make everything right. He said he saw Richard as merely an object that was in his way, like a table between them.

"I thought I was making love to them and if I did it right everything would be back to normal," he said.

Howdle was convicted of seventeen charges, including numerous counts of sexual assault, assault, and forcible confinement, for his vicious thirty-hour rampage. Though he had only one previous set of offences, the Crown applied for a dangerous offender designation, noting the chilling similarities with an earlier crime spree in May 1995. In that case, Howdle had sexually assaulted a woman after she ended their relationship. Released on bail, Howdle kidnapped one of the woman's friends, raped her and drove to Manitoba and back with her in the trunk of his car.

On July 9, 2003, in a Battleford courtroom, Clifford Barry Howdle was declared a dangerous offender and sentenced to an indefinite term in prison.

The decision brought cheers from Howdle's five female victims and Richard, who were all in court together, having formed a close bond forged by their common experience.

"Hopefully he'll spend the rest of his life behind bars, where he won't hurt anyone else," one of the women told reporters outside court. "I've already started the road to recovery and this will make it a whole lot easier."

"This is the happiest day of my life," said another.

The names Angie, Judy, Richard and Lorraine are pseudonyms. A court order prohibits publication of any information that would identify them.

JACK OF DIAMONDS

The translator arrived at the settlement that night. Louis Lavallee brought the whiskey, just as he'd promised, and as soon as he arrived, George took out the deck of cards. As Lavallee watched, George began laying the cards carefully on the ground, surveying each card with concentration before speaking aloud what the deck revealed. If the two men went out to the woods together the next day, George said, they would find the things Lavallee was seeking: The valise, the axe, and, most importantly, the answer to the question: Who killed John McCarthy?

* * *

John McCarthy was last seen alive on June 10, early in the summer of 1883. A neighbour found the old man dead later that month, McCarthy's body lying in a small stand of poplar trees, the side of his head knocked in and his jaw badly broken. There wasn't much left of the body by the time it was found, with the summer heat, scavengers and insects having exacted their toll, but McCarthy's friends knew him by his clothes, and by the way his front teeth had been worn down to nubs from clenching a pipe between them.

The old man's house was a tiny one-room shanty with a roof made of earth and hay, and signs of his violent death were everywhere. Dried blood was spattered on the walls and near the fireplace, and drops of it were sprayed on McCarthy's buf-falo overcoat. A tin cup and a loaf of bread lay on the floor, and a candle sitting nearby was marked with bloody fingerprints.

The murder was shocking to those who lived in the area, both because of the violence of the crime and because McCarthy was known to be a good man, a sober gent of reli-able character with no real enemies. He'd had a disagreement with a man about some hay a few months earlier, but the issue had been resolved amicably and the two were back on speaking terms.

With few clues to go on—and anxious to make an arrest in the high-profile crime—police officers investigating the case were understandably relieved a few weeks later, when an old woman who lived in the Cree settlement near Troy suggested they talk to one of her sons.

Mary Stevenson told the officers her son George could use a deck of cards to tell things he wouldn't otherwise know. Mary said George had used cards to find lost things in the past, and she thought he may now be able to use them to find a murder suspect.

Since George spoke only Cree, the police enlisted transla-tor Louis Lavallee to help with the investigation. Lavallee met George at the Stevensons' tent one evening in July.

"If you supply me with a pack of cards and some liquor, I will tell you how to find him that you are in search of," George told Lavallee in Cree.

George said it was easy to find a lost man with the cards, even easier than finding lost objects. Lavallee was interested, and promised an extra $50 if George could solve the crime.

The next morning the two men went together to McCarthy's shanty, where they found the dead man's valise, his axe and a five-dollar bill hidden in the woods nearby—exactly as George had predicted they would.

When Lavallee and George returned to the tent village, George again took out the deck, shuffled the cards and spread them on the ground before him.

"I'll cut the cards in three places ... and if the Joker is near the Jack of Spades I will be able to tell you what you're in search of," he said.

George took the first card from the middle pile. The next card he turned up was the Joker, immediately followed by the Jack of Spades. George laid all the cards face up in three tiers and stared at them silently for a while. He was looking at the Jack of Diamonds when he finally spoke.

"This is the murderer," he said. "I have never seen him, but could pick him out of a hundred persons, I am so sure. This man has but little hair on his upper lip and very red eyes."

"Was it in the day or in the night the old man was murdered?" Lavallee asked.

George said it was at night. Lavallee then wanted to know if the old man was asleep at the time.

"No," George said. "Sitting by the fire reading with a light before him, his back towards door. Door open, murderer went in. Old man looked behind, paid no attention, went on reading. Murderer took an axe that was standing by the door and killed old man. When you go into the house you will see the blood on the wall."

George said the murderer hit the old man on the head three or four times with the axe, then dragged the body into the bush. He said the murderer then ran back inside the shack, took his victim's valise and axe, and ran away.

"Opened valise and found $3 and that is all he got for murdering the old man," George said.

Though George Stevenson hadn't previously been a suspect in McCarthy's murder, the detailed and seemingly accurate information contained in his card reading caught the attention of police investigators. There was no evidence to link Stevenson to the crime but the details he provided fit many of the details of the crime scene, and his story sounded like a plausible description of the murder.

With little more to go on than Stevenson's own words, George and his brother John were arrested and charged with murder. The two men were tried about three months later.

At the October trial, the doctor who examined McCarthy testified the 62-year-old man had been hit repeatedly with an axe or a heavy stone, and said a small fraction of the injuries inflicted on McCarthy would have been sufficient to cause death.

McCarthy had $110 in bills inside his shirt pocket, all soaked with blood and stuck together, and an IOU for $84 owed to him by two men named Stoddard and Jones. The men had left the area and were originally arrested as suspects in McCarthy's murder—Jones was found in Medicine Hat, Stoddard in Winnipeg—but both were released after police charged the Stevensons.

The Stevensons did not speak at their own trial.

After two days of testimony before what was later described by justice officials as a jury of "intelligent settlers," the two brothers were convicted of murder and sentenced to hang on November 28.

Immediately after the verdict, work began on a scaffold to host the Stevensons' execution. It would be the first hanging in Regina, the new capital of the Northwest Territories, and the scaffold was designed as a smaller version of the gallows at London's notorious prison, Newgate. The Regina gallows were finished and waiting as the execution date approached, but some high-ranking officials continued to have nagging uncertainties about the guilt of the two men.

On November 16, Minister of Justice Sir Alexander Campbell recommended commuting the executions on the grounds that the evidence against the two brothers was "so circumstantial and on the whole so inconclusive."

A letter from the Lieutenant Governor to Ottawa also noted a large number of "halfbreeds and Indians" had signed petitions pleading for clemency in the case. Since most of those signing the petitions could not write, Joseph W. Chaser signed the men's names in bold black ink on their behalf—Young Horse, The Man that Stands Strong, Thunder Storm, He Talks like a Gentleman and They Are All Against Him—each man

Cah mar Stee ah, hee, ah Sty
Standing High,
Pehumy
Car Aou, Tar, Cut,
Young Horse,
The man that Stands strong,
Car, Ta, Pay couch, en,
Thunder Storm,
Nar, Hoog, He mou,
Hee Shimps Lodge
Heck e, Cheace,
Pea, Soe,
Nar, May, e, New,
Car, Celneut,
He Talks like a Gentleman,
They all are against him
Car Pay warke Say Sum
Pay Hee, such

Petition that circulated in 1883 to spare the lives George and John Stevenson. Source: Library and Archives Canada/ <http://www.collectionscanada.ca/db/gad/inv/013ile.htm> RG13, Justice, Series B-1, Volume 1420, File : 178 A & 179 A

making his mark with an ink 'x.'

The Stevensons' parents, John and Mary, also wrote to the government pleading for their boys' lives, saying their sons were not guilty of John McCarthy's murder.

"Hope and trust in God that the innocent will not suffer for the guilty," they wrote.

And the holes in the case were starting to widen.

In a statement to police in November, George said his brother was with a white man named Jack Thompson that summer, and described Thompson as a young fellow, clean shaven with no whiskers. George said this man had given McCarthy's coat to John, and showed George where the valise and axe were hidden.

"My reason for telling Lavallee I could tell by the cards was that Thompson had told me everything," George said. "Jack Thompson told me that if I would tell on the cards where these things were, no blame would be put upon me and no more inquiries would be made."

John gave a similar statement. He said Thompson had come north from the United States, and had been traveling around with the Sioux that spring and summer. John claimed Thompson had given him McCarthy's coat, instructing him to say he bought it from a white man on the street. John even had a receipt, written in English, which neither of the brothers could speak or write. The receipt said: "Stephens paid me Tomas Jackson $10.00 payment in full for coat." It was signed with the name "Tomas Jackson."

With this new evidence, the execution was delayed until December, giving authorities time to look for the white man Tomas Jackson or Jack Thompson. When December arrived and no new suspect had been located, the execution was pushed back another two months. In January 1884, police in Prince Albert arrested a man who fit the description of Jack Thompson, but officers later released him without charges. The Stevensons received another reprieve soon after, and a new date was set for April 3, 1884.

On that day, there would be no reprieve.

At a meeting at Government House in Ottawa, Prime Minister John A. Macdonald decided the police should not continue looking for another suspect in McCarthy's murder. The Stevensons would hang.

* * *

The brothers found out they were to die only an hour before their execution, a morning that broke "bright and cheerful," according to a special supplement about the execution put out by the *Regina Morning Leader,* the city's daily newspaper. The paper said the two men slept little, ate a light breakfast, and walked boldly to the scaffold, exhibiting no sign of fear.

"They had evidently made up their minds to face that grim monster we call death without quailing," the paper noted.

The men's hands and arms were pinioned by the executioner, and they walked to the drop unaided. The executioner wore a black hood; the Stevensons wore hoods of white.

The paper recorded the event: "At 7:45 the rope was adjusted, after which they kneeled on the trap through which a few minutes later they were to be hurled into eternity, to

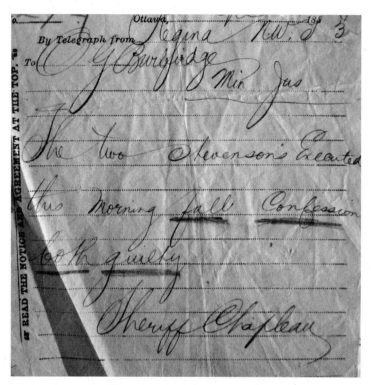

Telegram sent in 1884 confirming the executions of George and John Stevenson. Source: Library and Archives Canada/RG13, Justice, Series B-1, Volume 1420, File : 178 A & 179 A

engage in their last devotional exercises. Having completed these they arose, not a tremor being visible, kissed the crucifix which the priests held before their eyes and bade a final good-bye to all."

George convulsed for a moment before dying.

A telegram sent to Ottawa confirmed the news: "The two Stevensons executed this morning full confession both guilty."

During their time in jail, the men had given a few different accounts of who murdered John McCarthy. But two priests who were with the Stevensons the night before their execution said the brothers finally fully confessed to the crime.

Confessions written out in English by the priests and marked with an 'x' by both Stevensons recount the murder, and say the brothers robbed McCarthy then killed him because he was going to go to the police.

In the confessions, the Stevensons also heap praise on the officers who arrested and guarded them, beg forgiveness from God, and gushingly thank the priests for converting them to the Roman Catholic faith.

"I have endeavored to save my life by lying but now I am willing with resignation and even with joy to die for this crime instead of trying to save my life with another lie," George is reported to have said. "I trust my soul to the Almighty."

John apparently expressed similar sentiments, saying: "I willingly give up my life in expiation of my crime, I wish I could suffer still more to obtain the pardon I so much require … I am about to quit this world to appear before another tribunal where I hope I shall be judged favourably. No one else but my brother and myself is guilty of this crime, therefore look for no accomplices. Adieu."

John is said to have asked that the entire confessions be published, and in the moments before the executions, both brothers were said to have reiterated their guilt and again thanked the police officers, priests and jail guards for their many kindnesses.

Whether George and John Stevenson really said those things will never be known. The final words the men spoke were in Cree, and what they said wasn't recorded.

LOOKING FOR MARY CATHERINE

Sissie never forgot a birthday. She may have lived a more transient life than most, but her family knew that she always remembered special occasions. She sent home a card from Moose Jaw in April of 1983, but when months passed without another, and when there were no Christmas cards in December, her family knew something was wrong.

* * *

Mary Catherine Shanahan, or Sissie as she was known to her family, was a beautiful woman, slender with fine features, a quick wit and an artistic flair. She loved music, especially Motown, and won dance contests as a young woman in Chicago. Doreen Henahan-Bryan always thought of her sister as "charisma personified," a woman with a laugh so contagious you couldn't help but join in the joke.

But Sissie had been having trouble. It started in the early 1970s, when she was in her late 20s, and she soon started traveling to try to escape it, moving across the United States, and then up into Canada. Her family suspected Sissie might be schizophrenic, though she hid any problems when she talked to them.

"Everything was just rosy [with her]," Shanahan's other sister, Margaret Romeyn, would later tell a newspaper reporter. "That's kind of who she was. She would never tell you if she was facing demons or whatever ... The good things, she shared."

In January of 1983, Shanahan, then 37, sent a bank draft for about $2,500 from Moose Jaw to a cousin in the United States. It was an unusual thing to receive from a woman who had not worked steadily for several years, and had no apparent means of income. A note accompanying the bank draft did nothing to explain the situation. It read: "Please hold this but don't cash it. I am moving, when I get settled, I will write to explain. Love, Sissie. P.S. Smile."

A second $2,500 bank note followed within weeks and was accompanied by another mysterious message.

"Please hold this for me," it said. "I know I can trust

Mary Catherine Shanahan, 1970s. From missing persons poster.

you. I'm saving this for some medical treatment, which I need very badly. Don't worry, I'm OK. I'm hoping to be home in three or four months, I might be sending some cash for you to hold later. Put this draft in a safe place. There are a lot of potato chip suppers invested in this."

A final draft for the same amount followed early in February. In the accompanying note, Shanahan promised to write soon and acknowledged that her family may be wondering about the money she was sending.

"P.S. this will be the last one," she wrote. "I haven't robbed a bank."

Shanahan sent the birthday card two months later. It was the last time her family heard from her.

* * *

For almost twenty years, the disappearance of Mary Catherine Shanahan went without formal investigation, largely because of her transient lifestyle.

Mary Catherine's family conducted their own search, contacting health departments, women's shelters and churches, and even looking through Internet sites about serial killers and unidentified bodies. But they could find no trace of her.

The Moose Jaw Police Service's criminal investigations unit picked up the case in 2002, and it went through a couple of officers before being turned over to Corporal Cam Moore two years later. By then it had been more than two decades since Shanahan's family had had any contact with her, and the case couldn't have been any colder. Nearly all Moore could prove was that Shanahan had been in Moose Jaw for about a month in 1983.

"We don't have anybody, or any reason, for her to have been here," Moore told *Moose Jaw Times-Herald* reporter Suzanne Boyer late in 2005. "And then poof, she's gone."

The only clue was found on the three bank drafts Shanahan had sent home. Moore wondered why the name "Arlene Anhorn" appeared on the memo line. The family had never heard the name before, and the bank that issued the documents had never employed anyone by that name.

While researching her story about Shanahan, Boyer uncovered a crucial bit of information that she passed on to Moore: Arlene Anhorn's married name was Arlene Scheibner.

Contacted by the police officer at her home in Alberta, Arlene Scheibner said she had never heard of Shanahan, and hadn't gone by the name Arlene Anhorn for thirty years.

But she also told Moore that a fake income tax return had been filed under her maiden name in Ontario in 1987.

With that key bit of information, Moore was able to get a warrant granting him access to all the documents and records under the name Arlene Anhorn. Among the records were an arrest in Edmonton, health records from both Alberta and Saskatchewan, and a social-assistance application in Ontario— none of which related to Scheibner.

Some of the documents were signed, and handwriting analysis concluded the signature was likely Shanahan's.

The final record was from March 1987, when a woman identified as Arlene Anhorn died in a Toronto apartment and was buried in a numbered grave.

Information in medical records provided further evidence that Mary Catherine Shanahan had lived—and died—as Arlene Anhorn.

An amended death certificate was issued on January 5, 2007, nearly twenty-four years after Shanahan mailed a card home from Moose Jaw.

Even in the wake of the sad discovery, Shanahan's family hailed Moore for helping to find her after so many years.

"My sister wasn't a socialite or a debutante, she was just a sick person, and [Corporal Moore] looked for her like she was Princess Diana, when so many other people pushed us off," said Shanahan's sister, Michelle.

A statement released by Shanahan's family also urged agencies in the United States and Canada to devote more funding, personnel, and resources to advocate for missing people.

"The search for ALL missing people is important, not solely the wealthy, the famous and children ...," the statement reads. "Every human being is worth being searched for."

FATHER AND SON

He was the youngest in a family of eight, and though four other boys came before him, Stanley Gale Livingston Jr. was the one to be given his father's name. Shortly after Stanley Jr.'s birth in 1963, Stanley Sr. changed the name of his automotive business in honour of his new boy. The business had been called Three Star Service, but after that it would be Stan Livingston and Son.

* * *

After his parents separated, Stanley Jr. spent his childhood bouncing between them, going from his mother's places in Saskatchewan, Alberta and eventually B.C., to his father's little shack outside Sylvania. Each parent showed lots of attention to the boy, and spoiled him when he was with them. Stan Sr., who lived a rustic life in a small shack without running water, bought his son horses, a snowmobile, and a riding mower to play with. But despite the attentions of his parents, young Stanley was a troubled boy. He started drinking when he was still a child, pilfering booze belonging to his older brothers and sisters, or whatever other alcohol he could find around the house. By his early teens, Stanley Jr. was drinking nearly every day, using drugs regularly, and routinely getting kicked out of schools for his bad behaviour.

As Stanley's teen years wore on, his parents began to tire of the problems he caused, and Stanley, always used to having his way, started to get angry.

"I was spoiled and then all of a sudden as I got older and I wouldn't go to school and then it was beyond their capacity to control me, they gave up on me," he once complained.

He started telling people he felt like the black sheep of the family. He said it made him so mad that sometimes the only thing he could do was go out and destroy something.

As he neared 30, things weren't getting much better for Stanley Jr.. He still had a hard time holding down a job, was often in trouble with the law, and his relationship with his father was becoming increasingly strained. At times the two would get along, but more often their conversations degenerated into screaming matches.

Stan Sr. didn't agree with many of his son's choices, and he didn't approve of his son drinking, doing drugs and running around with a rough crowd. Having lost a lung and part of a lip to cancer, it also bothered Stan Sr. to see his son smoking so much, and he worried that the boy was ruining his own life.

Stanley Jr. didn't see it that way. He was tired of his dad hassling him about everything, and he was starting to resent the old man more and more. Stanley Jr. felt like his dad didn't treat him the way he treated other people, and didn't do enough for him. Sometimes his dad wouldn't even lend him money, even though Stanley Jr. knew his father had plenty of it.

Like others in the family, Stanley Jr. knew all about his dad's money. For years, Stan Sr. had been keeping carefully organized piles of cash in a briefcase or suitcase. Sometimes he kept it in the house, but usually it was in the trunk of one of the many cars parked outside. Stanley Sr. had money in the bank, too, but he always kept lots of cash around just in case.

Stanley Jr. thought about stealing the money for years. Once, he traveled all the way from B.C. to Saskatchewan to rob his father, but he got cold feet at the last minute and didn't do it. On another occasion, Stanley Jr. had everything in place to steal a car that held his father's briefcase of money, but once again, he couldn't bring himself to go through with the plan.

That his son was plotting against him couldn't have been a complete surprise to Stan Sr. Sometimes Stanley Jr. would threaten to burn down his house, to destroy his vehicles, even to kill him. The threats, made directly to Stan Sr.. and behind his back, started when Stanley Jr. was about 14 or 15, and continued with such frequency that after a while most people in the family didn't think too much about it. Stanley Woznia, a friend of the family, had been hearing it for years.

"Many times when he started talking and getting into it more he said he had no use for his father. 'I could just punch him out, I could kill him,' whatever," Woznia said.

Jodi Livingston was bartending at the Lion's Den bar in Prince Albert on a Friday night when his uncle, Stanley Jr., walked in. Stanley was with a friend, Les Roode, and the two men were in high spirits. They drank for a bit, then Stanley approached his 21-year-old nephew at the bar. Stanley told Jodi he needed money and was going to rob and shoot Stan Sr. to get some.

Your grandpa is old and it doesn't really matter, he told Jodi. Stanley called Jodi back later that night to say he had gotten a gun.

* * *

It was about four in the morning on February 13, 1994, when Stanley and Les got to the farm, banging on the door in the pitch black until the kitchen light came on and the 78-year-old Stan Sr. let them inside. Stanley and Les took their beer into the house and sat down at the kitchen table. The little house was as cluttered and messy as always, with wrenches, screws, and bolts scattered around the kitchen table where they sat. Stanley offered his dad a beer, but the older man refused. It irked Stanley Jr. that his dad wouldn't drink with him, particularly since he knew his father would sometimes drink with other people in the family.

Stanley Jr. asked his father if he could borrow $1,700 to buy a beaten-down truck that was for sale in Prince Albert. He'd asked for the money on the phone a couple weeks earlier, but at the time Stan Sr. had said no. The refusal made Stanley Jr. angry, and he had threatened his father, telling the old man to stay away or he'd hurt him. Now, sitting in his father's kitchen in the middle of the night, Stanley Jr. again pleaded his case for the loan. The truck was a little wrecked, he admitted, but it could be fixed up and resold. When his dad again refused to give him the money, Stanley Jr. blew up.

"Anybody off the street would come in and ask you for a hand, you'd be more than likely to help them," he said. "But with me, because I drink and I do dope and I'm a little rowdy, you don't figure I'm grown up enough to have responsibility."

Within minutes, Stan Sr. lay face up on the floor with two bullet holes in his chest, and Stanley and Les were back on the road, headed toward Prince Albert with $150,000 in cash. The getaway wasn't so smooth, with the two men driving into a snowbank not far from Stan Sr.'s place. Knowing he would be recognized by the locals, Stanley Jr. stayed in the backseat, covering his face with a blanket when Les went to get help. It took three farmers with a tractor to pull out the car, but eventually the men were freed. Les offered to give the farmers some money for their help, but the farmers refused to take anything for their time and trouble.

It didn't take long for police to arrest Stanley and Les and charge them with Stan Sr.'s murder. There was an obvious trail of evidence to follow, including the fact that Les had told the farmers where he worked in Prince Albert, and that the good Samaritans had given police a detailed description of Les, the car, and the person they saw hiding in the backseat.

When Les and Stanley got back to Prince Albert, they immediately disposed of Stan Sr.'s briefcase and the gun at the city dump, acting so suspiciously that the man working at the dump made a note of them. Then Stanley and Les did some errands around the city, first buying new tires for Les's car, then going to the mall to look for boots and shoes. Les also paid off a $70 debt at the bowling alley, pulling out a wad of cash with a thousand-dollar bill on the outside, and handing the alley's owner a hundred. "Have you ever seen a thousand-dollar bill?" Les asked the man.

Later, Stanley picked up a tasseled leather jacket he had left at a pawn shop. All the money they spent that day was marked in Stan Sr.'s distinct fashion, with his initials and a number inscribed carefully on each and every bill.

After the men were arrested, Les gave the police about $40,000 he had hidden in his mother-in-law's trailer. Another $100,000 was found in a drawer inside a room Stanley had rented under a fake name at the Twilight Motel.

* * *

Stanley went on trial first, facing a jury in a Melfort courtroom late in 1995.

Les Roode testified against his former friend during the trial, and each of the men blamed the other for the murder, claiming not to clearly remember the night through a fog of drugs and alcohol.

The defence admitted Stanley was an unlikable man—the kind of man you wouldn't want as a neighbour, never mind a son—but maintained it was Les Roode who committed the murder.

The prosecution argued that the second bullet, which tore through the old man's chest once he had already fallen to the ground with a fatal injury, showed Stanley Jr. pulled the trigger. The first shot was for money, prosecutor Gary Parker told the jury.

"What would motivate the second shot?" he asked. "Hatred would. Passionate hatred."

But in the end it didn't matter who fired the fatal shots.

Stanley Jr.'s planning, deliberation and intent were enough to make him culpable for the crime whether or not he ever touched the gun, and he was convicted of first-degree murder and sentenced to life in prison with no chance of parole for twenty-five years. Les Roode later pleaded guilty to manslaughter, armed robbery, and accessory to murder, and was sentenced to fifteen years in prison.

Fourteen years later, while serving time at William Head institution on Vancouver Island, Stanley Jr. was interviewed by a newspaper reporter working on a story about the loneliness inmates feel at Christmas time.

Livingston, then 44 years old, had helped organize some events to raise the inmates' spirits, including a special visiting day for families. He was particularly moved by the other inmates' daughters and sons.

"To see the little ones' eyes light up," he said, "that was Christmas for me."

BAD BLOOD

His clothes were shabby and his black suitcase battered, but he told the Regina cabbie he was pretty well off. He was going to Moose Jaw to work on a farm for the harvest, although he didn't really need the money, he said.

The same 35-year-old man with the steel-rimmed, rounded spectacles and prominent overbite showed up at the Moose Jaw taxi stand around eleven at night. This time, he told taxi driver James Keay his brother had died suddenly, and he needed to get to Saskatoon quickly to make the funeral arrangements.

As the men drove, the passenger said he was a bachelor who hadn't yet found the right partner, and that his wealthy father had recently died, leaving him a healthy inheritance. The cabbie saw the roll of cash the man had pulled from his hip pocket to pay the $45 fare. He had peeled off three $20 bills, still leaving a considerable sum in his pocket.

Keay's passenger climbed into the back seat a few miles outside Saskatoon and changed from his worn blue jeans into gabardine slacks. The gentleman and the cabbie parted company at the train station.

"Art Redcliffe" walked into the Saskatoon rooming house and paid for two weeks' rent. He needed time to recuperate from an appendectomy, he told the landlady. Then Art left shortly after paying.

House on the Petlock farm where five people were killed, August 30, 1955. Photographer unknown, courtesy *Regina Leader-Post*.

When he got into a cab in Saskatoon that Tuesday morning on August 30, 1955, he was a Manitoba farmer headed to North Battleford to find threshing work because his own crops had been hailed out. He asked the driver to shut the radio off because a soap opera was on.

He didn't like to hear the screaming women.

* * *

The two Mrs. Petlocks—Mike's mother Mary and his wife Angeline—were the first ones RCMP officers from Melville found, around five that afternoon. The wash, hung out a day earlier, was still blowing in the wind at the farm, just north of the tiny village of Fenwood. The blinds on the green and white, two-and-a-half-storey house were drawn and the doors locked. The sound of barking from the family's little black Pekinese drew the officers to the potato patch. That's where they found the women, lying partially covered by vines near the potato sacks they had been filling when the task was so abruptly ended, their hands still crusted with dirt.

The elder Mrs. Petlock had taken four shots to the chest. A fifth had struck the palm of her hand, likely when she had made a futile attempt to defend herself. Widowed six months

Petlock dog, which led police to find the bodies, August 30, 1955. Photographer unknown, courtesy *Regina Leader-Post*.

earlier, 72-year-old Mary had asked her son Mike and his family to move in with her in June.

Fair-haired, blue-eyed Angeline had indeed looked angelic in her lace and tulle wedding gown when she had married Mike almost four years earlier. On this day, her work clothes were covered in blood from the three wounds to her chest, shoulder and back. Powder burns on her plaid shirt suggested the shots had been fired at close range. The 21-year-old mother of two lay on her side with her knees drawn up to her chest, like the children she had once carried in her womb.

A small, pink coat had been left on one of the sacks of potatoes. A doll lay nearby on the ground.

Forcing open a window, the Mountie crawled into the locked farmhouse. Mike Petlock was face down on the kitchen floor. His lunch pail and cap were beside him, suggesting he had been killed shortly after arriving home Monday from his job as a section hand for the railway. Two shots to his head had stolen his life at age 34. A third bullet to the chest had been fired from less than two feet away. Like his mother, he had a defensive wound to the palm of his right hand.

Angeline and Mike's daughters were in a main-floor living room that had become a bedroom when the family moved in. Covered by a heavy feather tick, 3-year-old Dianne was barely visible on the double bed, but for her tiny foot, still in a shoe, hanging over the edge. A pea vine from the garden was twisted in her fine hair. Her sister Michaleen, 11 months old, lay on her back in the crib. Only her hand, extending upwards, appeared above the white sheet that covered her. The killer had fired two bullets into each girl, ensuring at least one struck their hearts.

Like their parents and grandmother, they had been killed by a .22-calibre repeating rifle. Some of the shots had been fired at close range, the muzzle of the gun less than six inches away.

"Methodical madness," was how one officer described what he had seen on the Petlock farm.

While the cold-blooded slaying of a family of five was incomprehensible, the motive seemed all too common. One of Mike's trouser pockets was turned inside out, his wallet emptied; and Mary's usually locked bedroom was ransacked. The family was rumoured to be "well-to-do." A lifetime of savings Mary had kept in a syrup can was missing. Mike's father Harry had never trusted banks. After his death, Mary had also kept their cash in the tin. She took it with her on the nights she slept at Mike's home, before he had moved in with her.

The syrup pail—minus its contents—and a man's blood-stained, grey shirt were found in Mary's bedroom. A single, long, light brown hair, resembling little Dianne's tresses, was stuck in the blood on the left shirt sleeve.

A report of a missing person is originally what brought the Mounties to the farm that day. And the missing man, Mike's brother John, was the one person they didn't find. When John Petlock hadn't come home from working in his fields, his anxious wife had alerted the RCMP. Officers found only a pitchfork near the stacks of ripened wheat.

The search for John Petlock intensified with the discovery of the bodies.

Mike's 1953 Meteor was found parked in Regina. The first real clue to John's whereabouts came from Moose Jaw taxi driver James Keay, who recognized a newspaper photo of the fare he had driven to Saskatoon.

The manhunt that stretched from Winnipeg to Vancouver ended quietly outside a rooming house in downtown Edmonton a week after the slayings at Fenwood. A landlady had become suspicious of her new boarder, who seldom left his room. A photo of a bespectacled man in the Edmonton newspaper finally prompted her to call police. Detectives were waiting as he left the house, walked a few feet, and removed his recognizable eyeglasses, tucking them in his pocket.

His landlady knew him as a Larry Hart from Brandon.

He gave his real name to the officers.

John Petlock had $11,952 stuffed in his pockets and packed inside his new, blue metal suitcase, his equally new name scratched on the top.

* * *

John's brother Walter and sister-in-law Gladys visited him at the Regina jail after his arrest and return to Saskatchewan.

"If I could have controlled myself after the first shot, I would have been all right," John said. Walter stopped him from saying more.

John would have plenty to tell a jury when he went on trial for murdering Mike.

"The plot is as old as Cain and Abel," wrote one newspaperman. Some said the friction between Mike and John went back several years. In the words of another of their brothers, "Mike had no use for John."

Others believed the troubles stemmed from their father's death in February. Clearly, tension was growing by the spring of 1955. In May, John and Nellie, then his wife of six months, left Mary's house and moved into one of their own on the outskirts of Fenwood. The next month, Mike and Angeline and their two girls moved in with Mary. Unfortunately, the new arrangement did little to settle the family quarrelling.

Resentments ripened over the settlement of Harry's estate. John believed he was being persecuted and shorted on his share. Mike thought John was angling to get more. Accusations flew that John had struck Angeline and his mother with a pitchfork in a dispute over some hay the day he moved out. John said it was a broom he had grabbed from her

John Petlock, Sept. 7, 1955. Photographer unknown, courtesy *Regina Leader-Post.*

hand—before she could hit him. In turn, John accused his brother Mike of taunting him that July, throwing stones and giving chase.

That same month, a friend remembered John coming home carrying a rifle and cursing, "God damn those bastards. I will shoot the whole works." John denied saying anything of the sort, explaining he had been out watching his cattle. One of his cows had mysteriously been shot in the pasture a year before, and that's why he had his gun. He had indeed borrowed a .22-calibre bolt-action Cooey rifle from his nephews a few weeks earlier. At the time, John said he wanted to shoot at dogs that were disturbing his chickens.

Their mother was pulled into the dispute. She was suing John to get back some farm machinery—equipment John insisted was his. Four hours before the shootings on the Petlock farm, John had met with his lawyer, who told him Mary was poised to launch further action to also take a granary. John did not wither with the news, but once again instructed his lawyer to take action in order to retain the disputed property. "Father gave me that granary," he insisted.

The story of bad blood between brothers became both motive and defence during the trial.

As the prosecution saw it, John had murdered the two women working in the potato patch, along with Dianne, who was a witness to the slayings. After shooting his niece, John had carried the child into the house, leaving a strand of her hair on his shirt; he then shot little Michaleen, and waited in the kitchen for their father to come home. Of course, this was only a theory.

The sole living witness to the mayhem was the accused.

And John had a different story.

John had heard shots coming from the farmhouse when he was stooking on the home quarter, preparing the wheat sheaves for harvest. As he approached the house, Mike exited with a rifle.

"You come for some medicine too," John quoted his brother as saying. They scuffled over the gun.

"I protected myself. He was going to shoot me," John said in a statement to police. The wrestling continued, the two men chasing each other around the chicken coop. When John finally got the rifle, it jerked and "accidentally the shot went off."

As John recalled, Mike kept coming at him, yelling, "Shoot some more! Shoot some more."

Later, he would tell a jury, "Oh God. I was completely out of control. My head was just like on fire, so I pumped two more shells into him."

John dragged his dead brother into the kitchen, changed out of his bloody shirt, and jumped into Mike's car, where he found a suitcase packed with money and clothes. Despite spending perhaps as long as two hours "roaming" the house—in search of a burglar, he said—John swore he knew nothing of the deaths of Mary, Angeline, Dianne or Michaleen until he read about them in an Edmonton newspaper.

Prosecutor William Rose was particularly incensed by the suggestion that Mike had killed his own family—and with John's borrowed gun.

"He had no reason for shooting his own children and his wife. This is a monstrous thought, against humanity and against reason," Rose told the all-male jury. He contended John's flight with his mother's money and all the lies told along the way were not the actions of an innocent man.

Defence lawyer Emmett Hall, who would become a judge in the Supreme Court of Canada six years later, attempted to plant doubt with a different theory: a tormented man who engaged in a "life and death" struggle with his brother. "He had a right to preserve his life," Hall said.

"By the grace of God he was not killed by that first bullet fired at him by Mike," Hall argued. At best it was self-defence, and at worst an accidental shooting, he contended.

The jurors did not accept John's claim of self-defence, but they also dismissed the Crown's theory that this was a premeditated murder motivated by revenge and greed.

After four hours of deliberations, the jury was convinced John's shooting of his brother was manslaughter, not murder. John was never tried for the other deaths.

When he had sat smoking a cigarette in his cell after his arrest in Edmonton, John Petlock had told an RCMP constable, "I guess I will be getting life for this."

But he reaped the benefit of the jury's lesser verdict. The judge sentenced Petlock to seventeen and a half years of hard labour in prison, one of the longest manslaughter sentences ever imposed at the time.

As Petlock was led from the courtroom, the soft-spoken man was heard to utter only one word: "Whew."

FEMALE AMBITION

Ralston and Sikorski were cruising in the south end of Regina one June morning looking for a grey car. According to the dispatcher, it was some kind of Dodge with a Saskatchewan licence plate. It sounded like the car was heading to the edge of the city, so the officers pulled over to the side of the Wascana Parkway and left their car running.

Corporal James Ralston and Sergeant Albert Sikorski were out of uniform that day, plainclothes and cruising in an unmarked car. When the Dodge passed, they slipped in behind it unnoticed, then radioed for backup. They stayed close until another unmarked police car showed up, then they put on their lights and sirens and forced the car over to the side of the road. Everyone skidded to a stop and Ralston jumped out, approaching the Dodge cautiously with his gun drawn.

There was a man sitting behind the wheel of the car. Ralston shouted for him to get out of the car and lie down on the road, which the man did immediately. Then the officers searched the man, put him into a cruiser that had pulled up, and sent him to the police station.

Meanwhile, Sergeant John Cavers grabbed the keys from the ignition of the Dodge, walked to the back of the car and opened the trunk. There was a woman inside. She was small and thin but still cramped and bent lying on her back. She was wearing a beige dress and no shoes. A purse at her feet was open and bursting with a wad of cash. She looked up at the officers.

"Shit," she said.

* * *

Beverly Ann Bishop was an ambitious woman.

She wanted things. Nice things, for her and for her kids. She was tired of always having nothing. She'd been working for the City of Regina a bit, but it was just casual work, not enough to pay all the bills, never mind buy anything extra on the side. Beverly didn't want to go back on welfare, but the bills were piling up. It takes a lot of money to run a household, and she was struggling. She had a plan she thought would work, but when she told her boyfriend Rodney she wanted to do an armed robbery, he thought she was crazy. Beverly wasn't deterred by his response. She didn't care much about his thoughts on it.

"Well, I'm going to do it anyway," she told him.

It was shortly before three in the afternoon on December 7, 1983, when the guy walked into the downtown branch of the CIBC bank. He was wearing a trench coat and a hat, with black gloves and a wildly bushy moustache. He strode to a wicket and passed the teller a brown paper bag and a note. It read: "Give me all of the money now."

The teller froze as the words sunk in, then quickly pushed a couple handfuls of cash across the counter.

Frederick Townsend was hanging up his coat when he realized the bank where he worked was being robbed. He looked down the counter and saw the man in the trench coat.

"Is that a man, or is it a woman with a moustache?" he wondered aloud.

Salesclerk Helen Forbes wondered the same thing a few minutes later, when a strange couple made their way through the second floor of The Bay. Helen nudged another clerk, who glanced up and saw the bizarre-looking couple; the little guy in a trench coat and hat, the tall man with sandy-coloured hair.

"Oh well, you see all kinds of things," Patti-Lou Taylor said with a shrug. The little guy was wearing some kind of crazy get-up.

"Patti, that's not a man," Helen said. "That's a woman dressed up like a man."

Beverly did another one in May, this time walking into a bank at Victoria Avenue and Park Street in a pair of overalls with a big bushy moustache and a hard hat. She carried a lunchbox, and pushed a note across to the clerk with a small, tanned, trembling hand. The note said: "Give me the money. I have a gun!"

Beverly tilted the lunchbox so the frightened teller could see the gun, and waited while the teller put a few handfuls of money into the box. Then Beverly said, "That's it. Good enough," closed the lunchbox and walked out.

As summer approached, the arguments between Beverly and Rodney were getting worse. He didn't like the robberies, and told Beverly what she was doing was wrong. He was afraid she was going to end up going to jail, but Beverly wasn't worried. She knew she was doing the right thing for herself and her family, so she gave Rodney two choices.

"If you don't want to help me with this then you can go home and pack your bags," she told him. "And I don't want to have anything to do with you anymore because you're not helping."

So Rodney helped.

Late on the morning of June 19, 1984, Linda Miller watched a peculiar-looking person walk through the doors of the Southland Pioneer Trust and head for Sandra Fyffe's wicket. The person was wearing overalls and a hardhat with a wig and a moustache. It was Beverly Bishop. She put a lunchbox on the table and passed Sandy a note demanding money. Sandy handed over some cash, and Beverly walked out.

Half an hour later, Rodney was lying on his stomach at the side of the road being handcuffed, with Beverly hiding in the trunk of the car. Beside her was a green garbage bag with a hardhat, coveralls, an air pistol, three wigs and a fake moustache.

At the police station, Rodney seemed confused about why he was under arrest. He wanted to see Beverly.

"If I could see her I'll show you that I'm not involved in this," he told them. "I haven't had anything to do with this. This wasn't my idea."

Testifying at her ex-boyfriend's trial six months later, Beverly completely agreed. She said she'd committed five robberies in Regina and a couple more in Saskatoon, and took responsibility for every single one of them. She dismissed the notion that Rodney may have made her do it.

"Him and I got into an argument prior to this because he didn't think that what I was doing was right, and I'm not one to be taking orders from the male species," she told the court and jury. "They tend to think that they like to have control over the women, but in my case I'm my own person."

"It wasn't him telling me, 'Bev, I want you to go out and do this,'" she said. "It was my own thoughts. Some men believe that women are not capable. Well, especially the police believe that it's highly unlikely for a woman to be able to sit down and put together a bank robbery."

She said Rodney had even warned her that she would go to prison for the robberies, but she'd ignored him.

"I guess I was too sure of myself and what I was doing, but Mr. Nelson didn't have any influence over me," she said. "Nobody really has much influence over me except myself."

It echoed what Nelson had been telling police all along.

Arguing his case alone before a jury of five men and seven women, Nelson explained why he helped Beverly rob banks even though he knew it was wrong.

"Because of the emotional feeling I have for her and the way I feel for her and to let her know I would stand by her through everything," he said.

The jury found Rodney Nelson guilty of aiding and abetting two bank robberies, and having $300 in stolen cash from one of the robberies. He got seven years in prison. Beverly Bishop, who had pleaded guilty to three counts of armed robbery before Nelson's trial, got four years.

"I'm the person that likes to do what I want to do whether or not someone is telling me this is right and this is wrong. I've always been that way, probably a stubborn streak ...," she said. "I'm ambitious, but maybe not in the right sort of ways that I should be ambitious. I'm learning that now, as I'm in the penitentiary."

ALONE

The man came from the west, walking in the centre of the tracks with the summer grasses growing high on either side. Every so often he would stop and look around as if he'd lost something, glancing back down the tracks and pausing for a moment before continuing his journey toward town.

When Frank Catlack finally got to the station at Patrick, he sat down on a bench by himself and waited for the train. He sat quietly, didn't say a word when Richard Caswell walked by and said hello. It wasn't Frank's reaction that got Richard's attention. Frank was a shy and reserved man, never outgoing at the best of times, and the two weren't really what you'd call friends. But Frank was usually with that woman, and this time he was alone. That's what was so peculiar.

Richard Caswell wasn't the only one to note the woman's absence at the train station that day. She was the kind of woman you noticed, after all, neat and smartly dressed with long dark hair and a pretty smile.

And they were always together. Always. They'd go to the store together, get the mail together, go into town together. They'd even applied for jobs together at the Plaza Hotel in Balcarres a couple of weeks earlier. Seeing Frank sitting alone at the back of the train as it pulled away from the Patrick station, Charles Alcock also wondered where the woman was. Before that day, he had never seen them apart. Charles didn't say anything to Frank about it, though, and when the two men spoke it was mostly about the hard work that would come with the approaching harvest.

When the train slowed to a halt at the Balcarres Station, Frank and Charles got off and went their separate ways. Frank went to the Plaza Hotel, checked in, and took a few beers back to his room. The two men saw each other again that evening at Al's Café, where Charles was eating dinner with some guys from work. Frank had been sitting alone at the counter, and stopped by Charles's table on his way out. Charles noticed Frank had deep scratches on his face and an ugly-looking gash on his hand. Frank was holding a cigar, and he asked if anyone at the table had a match.

Neighbours had started noticing the smoke that morning of August 16, 1948, a blue plume curling up into a cloudless summer sky. There was no wind that day, so the smoke rose straight up into the trees, already more than would come from a chimney and getting thicker.

* * *

Frank Catlack had spent his entire life in the Patrick area. At 39, he looked weary and worn, with a down-turned mouth and brown curly hair that was thinning and wispy on top. He had been to school a bit and could read fairly well, choosing mostly to read comics and the funny pages, but he was slow, and often seemed awkward and self-conscious. He'd been married as a young man and had a 12-year-old daughter somewhere, but he hadn't seen the girl for several years.

Frank met Florence when she was working in Regina in the fall of '47. He soon struck up a relationship with the pretty 20-year-old, at first hiring her to work for him at his farm, then lavishing her with gifts of clothing and jewellery—a watch, a signet ring, a silver bracelet with a nameplate. She was three months pregnant when they met, but the baby died of malnutrition soon after birth. Before long, Frank and Florence were living together like man and wife.

The first time the couple visited Florence's mother at her home outside Lebret, things were peaceful. Still, Marie Louise Brabant saw something troubling in her daughter's new boyfriend.

"I noticed that any time Florence went out, the accused would be peeping through all the windows in the house to see who she was talking to," she would say later, speaking to an interpreter in her French-Cree dialect. "I came to the conclusion that he was a jealous man."

By the next time Frank and Florence visited, in July, the strains on their relationship had become even worse.

"A day didn't pass but there was not a quarrel for sure," Marie Louise said. "Every day there was a quarrel, and sometimes for good measure a second quarrel came on."

Frank Catlack, 1948. Copyright Department of Justice. Reproduced with the permission of the Minister of Public Works and Government Services Canada (2008). Source: Library and Archives Canada/ Department of Justice fonds, RG13, B-1, Vol. 1674, file cc658.

Frank grabbed Florence during one of those quarrels but Mary Louise jumped in, her temper flaring as she saw her daughter mistreated. Later, Florence told her mother Frank had choked her once when they were at home on the farm. Florence said her neck was sore for days. And then, a month later, Frank's farmhouse burned down.

It burned on a Monday, smoldering hot in the morning, blazing angrily by the afternoon. Some people who lived in the area tried to fight the fire, but it was too big and out of control to do anything, and, in the end, they let it go.

The two-room farmhouse burned to almost nothing, reduced right down to its clay foundation. Looking down at the scene from the RCMP airplane, the house was a charred grey smudge on the vast patchwork of prairie, a smoking dot in the midst of all the crops shining green and gold in the August light. All that remained was a bed, a stove and a body.

Sergeant Robert Macara took charge of the human remains, putting the gruesome heap into a cardboard box and setting it carefully in the backseat of Detective-Corporal Gerald Carroll's car. The box was taken to Yorkton and stored in the basement of the RCMP detachment overnight, before being transported by plane to Saskatoon for the pathologist to examine.

Dr. Donald Moore could tell it was a female who had once borne a child. Other things were harder to determine. The remains were so badly burned there were no features left, and most of the organs had been cooked through by the extreme heat. It didn't look like the woman had been alive during the fire; that much, at least, had been a blessing. But judging from the deep fractures running across the woman's skull, hers hadn't been a peaceful passing.

A couple of days after the fire, an RCMP officer picked up Frank Catlack at the Plaza Hotel and took him to the RCMP detachment to talk. It was a routine fire investigation at first. Then Frank pulled out a $2,000 fire insurance policy he happened to be carrying with him in his pocket.

Detective Carroll had been at the Catlack farm all day, and didn't arrive back at the Balcarres detachment until late that night. He found Frank sitting in an armchair in the office with his hands over his face, picking at a series of angry scratches lining his left cheek. Frank said he needed some time to think.

The next morning Frank slept in and had breakfast before sitting down with Detective Carroll and Henry Hermanson, a former police officer who had recently taken a job as a fire insurance investigator. Frank asked the two men if they'd grant him a wish if he told the truth.

"What is your wish?" Hermanson asked.

"I don't want to live without her anyway," Catlack said. "Will you take me to Regina and hang me right away?"

His confession began like this: "We were really both too jealous of each other. I thought too much of her. She always said the same thing to me."

It had happened at about eight in the morning, he said, not long after they got up. It seemed like they were arguing from the moment they opened their eyes. Florence told him that if they weren't so jealous of each other, it would be all right. It was silly of them, she said.

Frank said he asked Florence if there was another man in her mind, but she said there wasn't, not ever. But something else was in there, a thought that bothered Frank just as much, maybe even more. It was a thought of leaving. Of leaving him alone. And that was the thought hanging between them when she spoke next.

"I don't know what I should do," she said.

He didn't let her say any more.

"I told her, 'if I can't have you no one else will,' and I told her, 'I am going to kill you,'" he remembered. She scratched him, and he hit her on the head with an iron pipe he used with the wood stove. Then he put his rough hands around her slender throat and squeezed tightly until she stopped struggling. He kept squeezing until her breath stopped, until he knew she would not leave him.

Frank left Florence's body lying on the floor by the bedroom door while he changed his clothes, ate lunch, and packed up some of his personal papers. He threw a lit cigar onto a pile of magazines and newspaper piled by the stove, and he noticed that the pile was starting to burn as he walked out the door.

Frank wrapped Florence's jewellery in a white scarf and hid the bundle along the tracks as he walked toward Patrick.

He later drew a diagram for police, and even took them to find the jewellery.

"I might as well tell you, I set the house on fire," he told Carroll and Hermanson, finishing his story. "I got nothing to lose."

Frank said he wanted to die, that he didn't want to live without Florence. A judge and jury were happy to oblige, finding Frank guilty of arson and murder and sentencing him to hang on January 14, 1949.

But Frank couldn't wait. A few hours before his execution, he committed suicide in his cell. Alone.

SEA OF FIRE

Fighting like a man possessed, Richard held his sword with his right hand and his shield with his left over his heart.

"Go ahead and shoot. Your bullets can't hurt me now," he shouted.

Richard had on his "full armour of God"—just as it said in the pamphlet he had received hours earlier. The leaflet, called "Satan on the Run," quoted Ephesians from the Bible where it talks about "the shield of faith whereby you can quench the fiery darts of the evil one" and the "sword of the spirit."

That's who Richard was—a soldier for God, protected by his "spiritual armour," and ready to do battle with the devil.

The man pointing his revolver at Richard put his gun back in his holster. Richard, standing in the living-room of his parents' farmhouse, was not armed—at least not with any visible lethal weapon. Quite certain he would one day be the star quarterback for the Saskatchewan Roughriders, Richard hurled chairs, vases and lamps at the intruder, an RCMP constable.

Richard was doing God's work. The officer in front of him and the two others who had taken his side were not. They were working for the antichrist.

"You're agents of the devil," Richard charged.

While Constable James Burns walked slowly towards Richard, one of the other officers came from behind, tackling the aspiring quarterback, and wrestling the wild man to the ground. All the while, Richard continued to yell, "Satan" and "begone."

Burns knew the young man on a personal level. That Richard was quiet and law-abiding. This was not the man he encountered that afternoon when he drew his sidearm. Burns asked Richard if he knew what he had done.

Without a hint of doubt or regret, Richard Charles Bieber replied: "I killed the devil."

* * *

Richard had his own house in Wolseley, but it no longer felt safe to him. At the start of 1982, he returned to his parents' farm, not too far from town. The 22-year-old spent New Year's Eve there alone listening to an album by a new Alberta rock band called Jenson Interceptor. The songs on the self-titled debut album, on the House of Lords record label, included "Freedom Fighting" and "Heavenly Angels." But there was one Richard particularly liked: "Crazy Monkey" with the words, "You'll be the next star quarterback." Richard was convinced it was about him.

He was as staunch a believer in that fact as he was in his new-found faith. Richard, baptized and confirmed in the Lutheran church, had drifted away from religion as a teen. His mother Bertha, a devoutly religious woman, was pleased when he started to show an interest again in the latter part of 1981. Richard had rediscovered religion through a television program and started to go to church regularly. He wanted to dwell on the Book of Revelation and its passages about the antichrist, the beast and Armageddon. Bertha tried to guide him towards the more inspirational Psalms and Proverbs.

A day after marking the New Year, Richard put his hand on his father's head and said, "In the name of God, cast these demons out of him." Thinking his son was in some sort of trance, Harold grabbed Richard's arm and asked what he was doing. "I didn't realize what I was doing," his son replied.

Richard's fears followed him to his parents' house. He was terrified to sleep in the basement or with the lights off. "When it's dark, that's when the demons are at work," he said. Bertha would stay up with him half the night, reading from her Bible and trying to comfort her firstborn son through prayer and spiritual guidance. Having done so for several nights in a row, she was exhausted by January 3, so her husband stayed with Richard in the living room. Richard sat in a chair reading his Bible until he eventually dozed off. Harold awoke to hear his son shouting for God's power. The noise awakened Bertha, who led her troubled son to her bed, where he promptly fell asleep.

At Bertha's request, Pastor John Koester came by the farm that day. He and another church member prayed with Richard. At one point, the minister began speaking in tongues.

"I was speaking in tongues because I didn't know exactly how to pray for him. I needed God's help and I didn't want my own mind to confuse the issue of what I thought might be needed, so I was asking directly for God's help," he later told court.

The minister met with Richard at his own house on January 4. Months later, Richard would tell his father how Pastor John had helped cast demons out of his cupboards, television, closets, bedrooms, and even his stereo, where he played his "Jenson Interceptor" album. The minister called it a "cleansing" and left Richard the pamphlet with the passage from Ephesians.

Harold was in Regina getting his truck fixed most of that day. He returned home in the late afternoon to find his agitated son pacing the house and fiddling with a screwdriver in his hands. Harold asked what was bothering him.

"Tonight, John Koester and I are going to kill the devil, defeat the devil and throw him in the sea of fire," replied Richard. Harold tried to reason with his son, telling him defeating the devil was God's goal. "Who is this devil?" asked Harold.

"Dad, you are the devil," his son answered. Richard recognized the devil by the number 666, just as it said in Revelation. He noticed his father had six children, six lamps in his home, and six chairs in the dining-room.

Harold told his son what a terrible thing that was to say. He wanted Richard to return to his own house. "No, I will never go back home," Richard said. Bertha suggested calling Pastor John, and Harold urged his wife to come with him. She refused, not wanting to leave her son alone because she feared he was suicidal. Bertha told Harold to go alone and get John.

"I love you," Bertha said as she saw her husband to the door.

Harold was certain his boy was beyond any help the minister could render. He made inquiries about having Richard committed to a mental institution, and stopped by the church. Harold, the minister, and a third parishioner formed a triangle, got down on their knees and prayed. At one point, Pastor John called on God to keep Richard from doing anything drastic. Harold became worried for his wife and went to phone the RCMP. The minister's wife ran into the room.

"Harold, there has been a terrible tragedy."

* * *

Bertha Bieber was beyond help when the officers arrived at her home and found her lying on the kitchen floor. They had been summoned by her son-in-law, who had come to the house to assist Bertha's youngest son.

The son had arrived home from work around 5 p.m. to find his older brother Richard sitting on top of their 56-year-old mother, with his hands around her neck, squeezing the life out of her. Together Bertha's son and son-in-law tried to pull Richard off, even going so far as to hit him on the head with a 7-Up bottle. Richard fought back, swinging a chair.

"I got the devil," Richard told them.

The mentally ill man would later tell psychiatrists how he believed his father was the antichrist. He grew frightened when his father tried to send him home because he knew his house was filled with demons. In Richard's mind, his father was controlling his mother. As mother and son sat together in the kitchen, Richard saw her face become distorted, and her voice man-like, as if the antichrist had transformed her. That's when he knew he had to kill her. He had to kill the devil or be destroyed himself.

His hallucinations about his mother were as real to him as the visions he had later in his jail cell, when he saw images of the devil, statues of hockey and football players, and a picture of the city of Jerusalem in pure gold. To Richard, the weightlifting equipment at the jail was a sign from God that he would become a star quarterback.

The doctors said Richard was suffering from paranoid schizophrenia. A jury acquitted him of second-degree murder, finding he was not guilty by reason of insanity. Upon hearing the verdict, his father quietly sobbed. Harold had visited his son several times at jail and the secure psychiatric centre where he was given anti-psychotic drugs.

"Richard realizes now that he didn't kill the devil; he killed a woman who was most dear to him," Harold had told the court.

Richard was once asked by a psychiatrist what he thought of his mother—the woman who, in his mind, had turned into the devil.

In her son's eyes, the doctor wrote, she was the "next thing to an angel."

TRAINS AND TROUBLE

The trains had direction and purpose; the boy who loved to ride them had neither. Keith was a drifter who showed up in Moose Jaw one day in July 1985 because that's where the boxcar he rode into town stopped. He lived under a bridge until Social Services placed him in a group home. Still he would wander, not in boxcars, but around the city's streets on his bicycle or his skateboard. Often, Keith would go where he could watch the trains. He loved how they could take you places, carry you away from trouble.

Troubled—that's what they often called Keith when he was a child growing up in Hamilton, Ontario. He would sit and rock and bang his head. Children's Aid became involved when he was 3. By the time he was 9, Keith's parents had split up. He grew up in foster homes. In his teens, the trouble turned to shoplifting, petty mischief, or failing to obey court orders. But there was the time he set a fire in an apartment stairwell after the caretaker had made him angry. Keith got a lot of attention for that. The law called it arson, and he was sentenced to a year in custody—to that point, his longest stint.

A few years after that trouble, the train carried him away to Moose Jaw. That's where he met Leo Johnathon Itcush.

Keith connected with six-year-old Leo. They both came from broken families. Leo too had spent a couple months in a foster home because he had been running away. And, like his new friend, Leo enjoyed spending his day riding his bicycle.

Unlike Leo, however, Keith was an adult.

Although Keith was childlike in appearance with his running shoes, T-shirts and ninety pounds that barely stretched over his frame, his birth certificate said he was 22 years old. The professionals put his age at closer to 12 or maybe even 14, intellectually and socially anyway, which suited Keith just fine. He liked being a child. He liked being with children. He would hang out with the other kids, playing in the park or exploring down by the river.

On August 2, 1988, Leo left home on his bicycle after the lunch hour. When he didn't return for supper, at first his mother thought he had gone over to his father's house. But as evening turned to night, Carrie became more concerned. Around 11:30 p.m. she called police.

Searchers scoured school yards, playgrounds, storm pipes and culverts for any sign of the four foot tall, blonde boy and his girl's bicycle, which matched his blue eyes. A tip about a boy talking to someone in a motorhome had police across Canada checking airports and border crossings. There was the promising report of a boy and an adult jumping a train— turned out it wasn't Leo. Someone thought they saw him in the West Edmonton Mall. A couple of psychics even offered suggestions. Every tip led to a dead end. Except the ones about Leo's friend Keith, the man who acted like a boy.

It was Keith's bike, not Leo's, that police found first. It was in a lot near the railyards. Keith, who had hopped a train out of town a day after Leo disappeared, was arrested for illegally crossing the border into the u.s. He was found on August 5 with only the clothes on his back—shorts and a T-shirt and a ball cap—and his skateboard. Keith returned to Moose Jaw, where police questioned him about Leo. Keith was supposed to come back to the police station again the next day, but he left, landing in Medicine Hat this time. As before, he returned and faced more questions. Officers lost track of him again after escorting him to Regina for a polygraph test. He ran from the police station and found another train, this one eastbound.

Leo's blue bicycle was not found until the morning of August 23, three weeks after anyone had last seen it or its rider. The bike was pulled from the Moose Jaw River, about five feet in from the bank. Another two hours would pass before Sergeant Merv Ellingson discovered Leo. An odour drew the officer to the thick brush on the river's edge, not too far from the picnic area at Maryland Park.

It was the smell of death.

Little Leo was still dressed in his white T-shirt, red socks and runners. His blue nylon track pants were pulled down over one hip. He had a red hooded windbreaker knotted around his middle. Its drawstring was tied around Leo's right wrist. His arms were outstretched as he lay on his side, but his legs were pulled up. Underneath one knee were a couple pairs of swim trunks. One had a name written inside the waistband, and it wasn't Leo or Keith.

The clothes were all intact, but exposure to the elements had taken a toll on the body, making it difficult to determine exactly what—or who—had caused Leo's death.

A railway worker finally caught the man-boy who loved trains. He recognized Keith Legere from a picture that was circulated around railyards across the country after Moose Jaw police issued a Canada-wide warrant. Keith was discovered hiding inside a caboose in the train yards at Thunder Bay, Ontario, a day after searchers found Leo.

While Keith never had much to say to the police officers he talked to in Moose Jaw, he opened up to Canadian Pacific Railway Constable Bruce Berringer, talking about the boy he had met at the swimming pool. The one he had ridden his bicycle with.

The one he had choked and hidden in the bush.

Keith was a little less forthcoming when he talked to a Thunder Bay police officer.

"I told them I might have," said Legere.

"Might have what?" the officer asked.

"Actually murdered someone, but I can't ever place myself murdering someone."

Keith said he and Leo were at the pool, Moose Jaw's Natatorium in Crescent Park. They rode down into the valley at the south end of the city. "He might have rode my bike, and we just got wrestling and went from there."

"I think I might have done something," he said, pausing. "I don't think I'd ever hurt someone."

But he had hurt Leo. Dental records showing blood in the teeth suggested the boy had died from asphyxiation. Keith had gotten into trouble two years earlier in Moose Jaw for choking a 13-year-old boy who had angered him.

That boy survived. Leo did not.

"When I left the pool, they said Leo was behind me. And I took him down in the bushes. We didn't do anything that had to do with sex. It was talk, ride my bike and things like that. And that he rode my bike for a while then I took him into the bush. We were wrestling and for some reason I started choking him and then he was moving around a bit. Carried him into the bushes and I hit him over the head with a log. I threw his bike in the water. I got scared and left."

"I think my intentions were to kill, but I don't know why they would be," he later added.

After Keith had picked up Leo's bike and thrown it into the water, he went to the group home for supper. When he did go back to check on Leo the next day, Keith thought the child's stomach may have been moving up and down, but Keith didn't tell anyone.

When questioned by police in Thunder Bay, he had insisted, "I don't really think I murdered anyone." The law agreed. Keith Robert Legere was allowed to plead guilty to the lesser offence of manslaughter. Justice George Noble said based on the sketchy information—provided by Legere primarily—about what had occurred, "The death of Leo Itcush was almost inadvertent."

Keith Legere, April 26, 1989, photographer Trevor Sutter, courtesy *Regina Leader-Post.*

Given Legere's troubled background and his intellectual and social shortcomings, "you get a picture of something akin to a disaster waiting to happen," Noble said. He sentenced Leo's killer to three years in prison. At the same time, the judge acknowledged, "our penal system does not have an appropriate institution or other means of dealing with the Keith Legeres of this world."

Behind bars, away from trains, Legere immersed himself in his other passion. He papered his cell with magazine pictures of young children. He watched Romper Room—and masturbated in front of the children's television show. Having failed to take any psychiatric treatment, learn to control his impulses, or gain any insight into his problems, Legere was denied parole. When he left prison after serving his full term, a corrections worker who feared Keith was still dangerous warned Moose Jaw's police chief.

But Keith didn't stay in Saskatchewan. He headed back home, to Ontario. The trouble began again, just a month after his release. He was arrested on May 30, 1992 for trespassing at Toronto's posh Royal York Hotel. His bail conditions ordered him not to communicate with children. Keith took a subway train downtown and was free only three hours when officers, who had him under surveillance from the moment he left court, saw him crouching down in front of two young boys near an escalator. Legere's bag held magazine pictures of young children, a screwdriver, water pistol, and a new pair of girl's panties.

He was acquitted of trespassing, but Leo Itcush's death became pivotal in Legere's trial for breaching bail conditions. Unlike the judge in Saskatchewan, Justice George Ferguson concluded Leo's killing indeed had a sexual element. He called Legere "a dangerous pedophile" who was at risk of abusing a child, even if his record contained no convictions for sex crimes.

"If I release the accused at this time, then I could never, ever face the parents, family or friends of some child harmed by the accused at a time when I had the power to keep him in custody," Ferguson said. Giving no credit for the eleven months of pre-trial custody, the judge sentenced 27-year-old Keith to the maximum: two years less a day in jail and three years of probation. Keith had already been released—and re-arrested five days later on new breach charges—when an appeal court overturned that sentence and conviction.

While in jail, Legere had collected pictures and newspaper stories that caught his interest: an encyclopedia page of a bare-chested boy panning for gold, a picture of Mickey Rooney as a child actor, clippings about the murder of a two-year-old boy in England, a photo of three young boys in hockey uniforms, and an item about cutbacks to transit lines. Some pictures of children were stuck in Playboy and Penthouse magazines.

Keith did get out again. And again, he found it difficult to stay away from children. After he was caught in 1995 wading in a park fountain towards two little boys sitting on a bench, Keith was put under yet another probation order to stay away from children.

Keith had always liked children, almost as much as trains. When children landed Keith in trouble, the trains carried him away.

THE ETHICS OF PURCHASING

Running a library is not easy. Running forty-six of them, forty-six small, under-funded libraries spread out in towns and villages around west central Saskatchewan, well, that is an even greater challenge.

Faced with such a task, Bruce Cameron couldn't help but see himself in somewhat mythic terms.

"Being the executive director of a regional library system in Saskatchewan often times reminds one of Sisyphus," Cameron wrote, in his 2002 annual report on the Wheatland Regional Library System.

Having held the executive director's position with Wheatland since 1971, Cameron was fully aware of the challenges. Some of Wheatland's libraries were squeezed into town offices or rec centres; one even fought for space inside a small gas station. Other library locations had crumbling infrastructure, and there were never enough dollars—let alone books—to go around.

Still, Cameron did his best, even penning a report called "The Ethics of Purchasing," which outlined the rigorous ethical practices he believed should be maintained within Wheatland. In the report, Cameron took a hard line on accepting perks from publishers, and made it particularly clear that a librarian should never take anything for personal gain.

"Not only must an ethical purchasing standard be maintained, but it must be *seen* to be both ethical and maintained," he wrote.

But in 1990, after two decades of toil, Cameron had finally found a way to make his burden lighter.

* * *

Bruce Cameron was on vacation early in 2004 when members of Wheatland's executive committee got an anonymous tip advising them to take a closer look at Desert Rose Books, a Nevada-based company Cameron had been dealing with for many years.

The board hired a private investigator, who soon discovered that Desert Rose Books and the company's owner, Herbert B. Cochrane, were pure fiction. Bruce Cameron was Herbert Cochrane, and it was Cameron who had registered Desert Rose as a company two decades earlier.

In reality, Desert Rose Books was little more than a name and a mailing address. Wheatland had never received any books from the phoney company, and the only person who had profited from the deal was Cameron, who had used his alias to steal up to $1,000,000 from his struggling library system.

The plot was relatively simple. Cameron would place phony orders with Desert Rose, then send real payments to Carson City, Nevada. The money would then be routed to a post office box in Richmond, B.C., and from there it would move again, this time traveling east to Saskatoon, where it would finally be delivered to an address on Circle Drive, and back to Cameron.

An audit found that of all the books Cameron bought for Wheatland in 2003, only about seven per cent were actually received by the library, and, of those, none had come from Desert Rose. The books that had been received were mostly discounted remainders sold by the crate, topped up with some cheap, bulk-purchase paperback bestsellers. Since the fraud had gone on for fourteen years, doing a complete audit of what was missing would have been an almost impossible task. It was a surprise twist for those who knew Cameron, who had previously been regarded as a dedicated employee with the best interests of Wheatland at heart.

"As a librarian, we're usually not greedy people. We really don't do it for personal wealth," said Rena Bartsch, who took over Cameron's position with Wheatland after he was fired. "What he did is astonishing to the library community."

Cameron was charged with fraud. Appearing in Saskatoon Provincial Court in May 2008, he pleaded guilty to stealing $497,503—though many believed the actual amount Cameron took was closer to $1,000,000. The author of his own misfortune, he paid back $500,000 to the library system in a civil agreement by selling his house and cashing in his pension and other investments.

When Cameron appeared in court again for sentencing in August 2008, Crown prosecutor Gary Parker said there was little explanation for the sophisticated scam.

"The motivation appears to have just been one thing, and that is greed," Parker said.

But defence lawyer Andrew Mason said Cameron had also paid dearly for his crime, finding himself at age 65 with no money and no assets, living in the basement room of a friend's house.

"Had he thought about this and thought about the implications, he would never have done it. It has destroyed his life," Mason said, calling the consequences "significant and catastrophic."

"It has brought shame and dishonour upon his name and reputation and has negatized all the good things that he did, which I think are considerable over the 34 years that he was associated with the Wheatland Regional Libraries," he said. Mason said the only positive thing in Cameron's life was a promising new relationship that had blossomed with a woman in B.C..

Judge Barry Singer accepted the lawyer's joint submission for two years less a day in jail, telling Cameron: "Only a person with a good reputation can commit a crime like this."

Cameron didn't say a word as he was taken into custody, and his expression was very hard to read.

LADIES' MAN

It was a wonderful time to be in Regina. The city was hosting the 2003 Grey Cup, and everyone was excited about the big game. The hometown Roughriders weren't even playing in the championship game that year, but no one cared. The party was almost as good as if they were. He was at a bar that night, hanging out with friends and enjoying the scene when a woman emerged from the crowd and walked toward him. He strained to hear her above the din of the room, but when she finally said those words everything else faded instantly away.

"You should get tested for HIV," she told him.

* * *

There were a lot of women in his life, each different and attractive in her way. There was Tamika, his wife and mother of his two little girls. There was Lana, beautiful and smart in B.C., and there was Jennifer in Montreal, always so loving and supportive.

In Regina, there was Christie, fun and wild and always up for a good time, and there was Tonya, who loved him enough to do anything for him. And there were more. There was the waitress, the nurse, the girls at the bar, and still others after that.

In the middle of it all, there was Trevis.

Trevis Smith was born and raised in Alabama. He played college football with the Crimson Tide before being signed as a free agent by the Saskatchewan Roughriders and heading north to Canada.

In Regina, Roughrider players are more than sports celebrities—they are icons and heroes, commanding legions of adoring fans and admirers in a province that is passionately devoted to its team. Knowing this, Trevis did his best to give something back to the community by volunteering with local charities, coaching high school football, and always making time for his fans. An intimidating man on the field, Trevis was unfailingly polite and approachable in his day-to-day life, and was well-liked by his teammates, coaches and friends. Trevis also enjoyed the company of all the women in his life and he treated them well, traveling with them, buying them gifts, making each one feel like she was the only woman in the world.

When Lana met Trevis, she knew that dating a professional athlete could be trouble. But though she was initially hesitant about getting involved with the handsome CFL player, her defences soon melted away. He was sincere and doting, and he called and saw her so often she couldn't imagine where he would even find time for any other women.

Still, sometimes Lana had her doubts. Once, after flying into Regina for a surprise visit in August of 2004, she became suspicious of Trevis and, while he was at football practice, searched through his house looking for clues he was seeing other women. When she found a pamphlet entitled "Living with HIV," she panicked. Lana went straight to an HIV clinic to be tested, and was nearly hysterical as she waited for the results. When the rush tests came back negative a few hours later, Lana immediately felt guilty for not trusting her boyfriend.

When Trevis got home, Lana told him she had gotten tested for sexually transmitted diseases after finding a picture

Trevis Smith, April 19, 2006, photographer Don Healy, courtesy *Regina Leader-Post*.

of another girl in his house. Trevis was annoyed at what she'd done, and told her she should have asked him before going for the medical tests.

"[He said] I shouldn't have just gone ahead and done that," she would remember.

Lana apologized, but she continued to have nagging doubts about what seemed to be a perfect relationship.

The couple had just returned from a romantic trip to Las Vegas in the spring of 2005 when Lana dialed a phone number she found on Trevis's cell phone. The woman who answered claimed to be Smith's girlfriend, and asked Lana if she knew that Trevis was HIV positive. There was something in the woman's tone that made Lana think she was telling the truth.

Back in B.C., Lana immediately got tested for HIV. When the tests again came back negative, she called the police.

* * *

"Hard." That was how Trevis's wife, Tamika, would describe their marriage in front of a hushed courtroom in Regina nearly two years later.

"Hard," she said. "It was a rough marriage."

Trevis Smith had been arrested at his home in Regina in October 2005 and charged with aggravated sexual assault for having unprotected sex without disclosing he had HIV, the virus that can cause AIDS. The charge is based on the notion that people cannot fully consent to sex if they do not know they are being put at risk for the potentially deadly virus.

The first charge related to Smith's sexual contact with Lana, and RCMP in Surrey, B.C. released a rare public warning.

"Normally the RCMP would not disclose the medical health status of a person who is charged with a criminal offence. However, in this case, the RCMP would like to issue a public warning as Trevis Smith is HIV positive," Constable Mark Searle said in a statement released to media at the time. "Anyone who may have had sexual contact with him and is concerned about exposure of HIV should immediately see their doctor or go to a clinic for testing. You are also asked to contact police in relation to this investigation."

Christie, who had a casual sexual relationship with Smith for several years, went to the police after seeing a story about Smith's arrest on the news. A second charge followed soon which named Christie as a victim.

Finding out Smith had HIV was devastating news for Lana, especially because she had planned to be a living kidney donor for her ailing father. Smith knew about her plans, and had even gone to visit her father in B.C., bringing him a Rider hat and T-shirt as a gift. Though Lana's HIV test came back negative, the transplant had to be delayed for a year to ensure she would not test positive, a delay which put her father's life in jeopardy.

Lana approached Smith at a football game in B.C. shortly before his arrest, sobbing as she faced her former lover.

"If you know how it feels to have it, why would you wish that on someone?" she asked him.

"I'm sorry. I was scared," was all Trevis could say.

Interviewed by Regina police in September 2004, Smith

admitted he had tested positive for HIV a year earlier, but maintained he had twice tested negative—including by a "freelance doctor" in Alabama.

"You're in a sort of a celebrity status here in town ...," said Corporal John Walker, also a former Roughrider, during a taped police interview with Smith. "There are girls out there, just like when I was playing, that wanna get with a Rider."

* * *

Trevis wore a mustard-coloured suit and a stony expression during his trial at Regina Provincial Court in February of 2007. Everything was on the line for him. His career, his relationships, and his freedom were all hanging by a thread. He looked tense and angry.

Smith's wife, Tamika, came to court every day of the trial, and sat with a small group of women in the front row of the public gallery. The two exchanged quick smiles at times, and were sometimes able to speak briefly before or after court.

Both Trevis and Tamika stared hard at Lana as the 26-year-old sat down to testify against her former boyfriend. She told court about their long relationship, and about the many times she had unprotected sex with Smith after he would have known he carried the HIV virus. During Lana's testimony Smith would at times shake his head, or jot down notes on a pad of paper.

During cross-examination, Smith's lawyer, Marie-Helene Giroux, chastised the woman for her behaviour.

"Why would you trust him ... when you have all the clues in the world?" she asked.

"I didn't think someone would be so malicious," Lana answered.

When it was Christie's turn to testify, the 31-year-old admitted she'd heard rumours that Smith had HIV, and said she asked him about it one night in the summer of 2005.

"I asked him if it was true, and he said no it wasn't true, that if he had it I would have had it years ago," she told court.

She said they had unprotected sex later that night.

As the Crown's case came to a close, Smith's lawyers decided to have him testify in his own defence. Sitting in the witness box, the powerful football player spoke so softly he could barely be heard. Smith said he understood how deadly the HIV virus could be, and said he was so careful he even kept his toothbrush away from his young children.

Smith said he told Lana he had tested positive for HIV, but she wanted to continue their sexual relationship even after she knew. He said Lana only went to the police after she realized he wasn't in love with her.

"She said, 'I'm going to make you pay for ruining my life,'" he testified.

Smith said he didn't have sex with Christie at all after finding out he had HIV.

In her closing arguments, Smith's defence lawyer described Lana as a "suspicious and snoopy person" who was motivated by vengeance. Marie-Helene Giroux said Christie may have made up the allegation for attention or to get money, and urged Judge Kenn Bellerose to look beyond Smith's infidelity when weighing his testimony.

"Mr. Smith is a frivolous man. He had a lot of women in his life ...," Giroux told court. "But this is no reason to disbelieve him."

But less than a week later, in the same Regina courtroom, Judge Bellerose found Smith guilty as charged, and said he would be considering a significant penitentiary term. Smith showed no reaction to the verdict, and gave a slight smile and a small wave to his wife as he was led from the courtroom. Minutes later, Tamika wept on the courthouse steps, and told a throng of reporters she was devastated by the verdict.

"We have two small kids that I have to explain [to] that Daddy is not coming home," she said.

Appearing in court again two weeks later for sentencing, Smith made a brief statement.

"I'd just like to start by saying that for this I apologize to this province, to the team that I represented for the last seven years ... I also want to apologize to the women I was involved with during this time, and my wife, for just my actions, and I ask that she forgive me for me committing adultery," he said.

Though neither Lana nor Christie tested HIV positive, Crown prosecutor Bill Burge described Smith's behaviour as "beyond recklessness."

"It's the deliberation that really aggravates this ... Mr. Smith carried this out knowing the nature of this illness and what it can do to a person," Burge said.

Bellerose sentenced Smith to six years in prison.

And as the 30-year-old former football star began his trip to the Prince Albert penitentiary, there were the many women in his life, each with her own view of what had happened, each processing the verdict in her own way.

There was Tamika, in Regina, vowing to stand by her husband, and Jennifer, in Montreal, still clinging to the idea of a future with Smith. And there was Lana, at home in B.C., glad to move on without him.

"I honestly feel ten pounds lighter," she said. "Finally I can close this chapter in my life."

Smith was granted full parole two years into his six-year sentence.

The names Lana, Jennifer, Christie and Tonya are pseudonyms. A court order prohibits publication of any information which would identify them.

UNCLE GEORGE

lthough the well near the blacksmith's shop was not supposed to be in use anymore, anyone could tell the nails had
recently been removed. With help from the town overseer,
who also happened to run the local lumberyard, William Whybrow pumped about twenty feet of water from the abandoned
well. Then they sent down a hook on the end of a rope.

Nothing.

The two were undeterred, certain the well was not the only
thing that had been abandoned.

Constable Whybrow, of the Saskatchewan Provincial
Police, wrapped one rope around his body, and another on his
foot. He made about five trips down, bringing up pieces of
wood and a sack of bricks.

When he snagged a bundle of clothes, Whybrow knew for
certain they were getting closer. The cloth coat had a distinc-
tive astrakhan fur collar, hinting at the wearer's Russian
heritage. Remarkably, a pin stuck into the lapel was still intact.
A pair of pants, another coat, and suspenders followed.

Finally, Whybrow found a foot.

With two more trips into the well, the officer fastened the
ropes to the body. It was nearing three in the morning on April
10, 1918, when they finally hauled up a corpse.

A sack over the head reached all the way to the knees.
He—apparent once the sack was removed—still wore his

trousers but only one sock, accounting for the foot Whybrow had seen.

His head had three cuts: to his cheek, the bridge of his nose, and his forehead. There was also a bruise on his neck, like someone had put some pressure on it.

Clearly, 70-year-old Mike Morowski had not left Elstow the previous month. Here he was only one hundred and twenty yards from his two-room shack, the last on the village outskirts, where he had been living for the past year.

* * *

The panic was evident on the little girl's face. Helen had never been to such a big city. Winnipeg was a maze of unfamiliar buildings and people and languages. She had wandered away from Uncle George and her sisters, and now the nine-year-old was lost.

A police officer recognized Helen's distress, and the child ended up in the care of a kindly matron at the police station. Helen could barely speak English. The matron could barely manage in Ukrainian. But somehow each knew enough to lead police officers to comb the hotels in search of Helen's uncle.

They eventually found him at the Savoy. Uncle George fetched Helen from the police station.

Earlier that day at the hotel, Helen and her sisters, 15-year-old Katie, and 13-year-old Nellie, had watched Uncle George count his money. There was $1,200, mostly tens and twenties.

Katie spent that night with a friend they had bumped into in Winnipeg. Mrs. Courgie had known the family when they farmed in the Colonsay area, back in Saskatchewan, and was surprised to see the girls in Winnipeg.

The next morning, Uncle George came by the friend's rooming house and gave Katie another $60—she'd already received $40 on the train to Winnipeg—to take care of her sister Helen. Nellie would travel with George to Prince Albert, where he was headed on business. George needed a passport to get to the United States, but he knew no one in Winnipeg to vouch for him.

He should have thought of that before he left Saskatchewan. But George Stanko had been in a hurry.

Six days later, George and Nellie returned to Winnipeg. George had his passport and train ticket to Buffalo, New York. What he didn't have was Katie and Helen. He headed to the rooming house to retrieve the girls, and got talking to the landlord. The man had overheard the girls discussing their father's missing money, and he urged George to return it. But Stanko explained that the money had been given to him to care for the girls upon their father's death. The landlord offered to help, explaining that he was also a lawyer. Stanko turned over $500.

It wasn't long before he had second thoughts. But the "landlord-lawyer" was no longer in the mood to help.

Stanko ended up at the Winnipeg police station, accusing the landlord of stealing his money. Detective William Smith took his statement around noon on April 9, 1918. It really was a sad tale—a father dead, their uncle put in charge of their care and money, now robbed. But Smith thought there were a few holes in the story.

By that time, Mrs. Courgie had brought the girls to the police station. Katie found a sympathetic ear and a recognizable tongue in one of the officers, who spoke several Slavic languages.

The teen told how she and her sisters had come home from school on March 27 to find their father counting his money. Having sold the family farm at Colonsay for $1,200, he had collected the last $100 instalment that February. Katie helped her father count his money on the kitchen table. There was fourteen hundred, mostly tens and fives. Mike Morowski tucked it safely into the money belt he wore around his middle.

As spring approached, their elderly father was making plans to head to North Dakota, where he had a brother. The girls' mother had disappeared from their lives eight years earlier when she left Mike.

While not a blood relative, George was really the only family they had. He had worked on the farm nearly seven years, and the children thought of him as an uncle. Other than his adopted family, George never really had much. He had worked sometimes as a porter at the hotel. At the lumberyard, he got paid twenty cents a ton for unloading coal. He still owed his employer $1 after taking a $5 advance on his pay. He was supposed to stay behind in Elstow when the family moved, but later people would recall seeing him with a roll of bills in his hands at the train-ticket window.

Mike had been busy organizing his life. He had sold the tiny shack. His eldest daughter Annie had recently married. Mike had plans for Katie to marry as well—but she didn't share them. Katie wanted no part of her father's choice in mates, preferring instead to stay with her younger sisters.

She was in the bed she shared with Nellie and Helen when a commotion in the next room awoke them sometime after midnight. Katie tried the door to get to her father, who was crying out, but the hook was locked on the other side. Climbing onto a trunk that was atop a box, she spied through the edges of the hole that fed the stovepipe into their room from the kitchen.

In the candlelight she could see her father taking off his boots as he sat at the table. Stanko was standing over him with her father's hammer in his hands. Katie's two sisters joined her on the trunk, catching glimpses of what would be their father's final moments. The children saw Uncle George strike their father's head, sending the old man sprawling to the floor. He tried to get up and get outside, but Stanko grabbed Mike by the hair, pulled him back inside and pinned him down on the couch.

As Stanko choked their father, the girls yelled out from behind the wall and pleaded for his life.

Mike Morowski said goodbye to his daughters.

Uncle George had other words for the girls: "Shut up or I'll kill you too if you don't keep quiet."

Stanko pulled off their father's clothes to get the coveted moneybelt. Then the man they thought of as family, indeed sometimes they had even called him "papa," stuffed their father head-first into a sack. He loaded the body onto a sleigh. Through a window by the light of the full moon, the girls saw the sleigh round the skating rink and stop behind the house at the well. Stanko lowered the body.

The girls pretended they were asleep when the killer returned and checked on them.

Early the next morning, Nellie asked Stanko about her father.

"He is very sick. He has gone to the hospital on the midnight train," Stanko replied.

"Don't tell us lies," Nellie fired back, pressing Stanko. He admitted their father was in the well.

That same morning, having stolen their father's life and life savings, Stanko kidnapped the dead man's daughters and boarded the train for Winnipeg.

By the time Winnipeg police searched him, only $461.40 of the missing money remained.

If the "landlord-lawyer" had truly stolen from the thief, he was never charged. On the train back to Saskatchewan to face a trial for his crime, Stanko blamed 15-year-old Katie.

"She asked me two or three times to kill her father because he abused her. He used to beat them up," he told police. Katie denied Stanko's claims when her turn came on the witness stand.

A partial cave-in halfway down the old abandoned well had kept Mike Morowski's body from falling the full ninety-foot drop to the bottom. His killer would not likewise be spared from the drop he faced five months later on a scaffold in Prince Albert.

MANHUNT

I t was dinnertime when the two RCMP officers pulled into the
yard. The fall of 1970 had been a bit warmer than usual, and
after a rainy morning, October 9 had turned clear and mild.

The house was near the small town of Macdowall, a couple
dozen miles south of Prince Albert. It sat right on the edge of the
forest, with a wall of trees growing thick and high around it, making the home feel even more secluded than it was already. The call
was all too typical when it came in—a domestic dispute between
an area farmer and his wife—and the two officers arrived at the
property expecting the usual kind of family squabble.

Both men were experienced officers. Sergeant Robert
James Schrader was the older of the two, a 41-year-old veteran
on the force with more than two decades as a cop. Though just
30, Constable Douglas Anson had already been a police officer
for eleven years.

Anson was walking toward the house when the first shot
hit him in the stomach and sent him spinning. A second shot
ripped into his back. There had been no warning, no confrontation, just the two shots, and Anson crumpled and fell on
the front step of the farmhouse where he had been standing a
moment earlier.

Schrader was at the side of the house looking at the truck
when he heard the first shot cutting through the crisp autumn air.

Another shot followed. Peering cautiously around the side of the house, Schrader saw his partner lying on the ground, and, realizing what had happened, ran into a grove of trees behind the house for protection. He had no other option—he had left his revolver in the car.

Schrader hid behind a tree, and was crouched there when he saw a child wandering through the yard. He emerged from his hiding spot and was motioning for the girl to take cover when the shooter spotted him and fired.

Schrader wasn't hit, and he tried to get even lower, trying desperately to hide himself from the marksman holding him in his sights. But a second shot found its mark, and a third left the officer lying lifeless on the cool ground.

Once Stanley Wilfred Robertson knew the two RCMP officers were down, he got into their police cruiser. Armed with their revolvers, a high-powered police rifle, and a police radio, he sped toward the bush.

Robertson's wife was almost hysterical when she called the RCMP and told them what had happened on the farm. Then she fled to a neighbour's house with the couple's eight children, knowing her husband might be looking for her—and the children—next.

Stanley Robertson didn't seem so dangerous. The 40-year-old was short with a slight frame and a quiet manner. But it was clear from the start that he was not going to be an easy man to bring into custody.

The area was dense, full of wildlife, largely untrespassed. Robertson was born and raised in that area, and he knew the woods well. He was also an excellent trapper, an experienced woodsman and a crack shot with a rifle. He was heavily armed, and he was extremely dangerous.

As the RCMP mobilized, veteran Prince Albert police officer W.H. Preston realized what searchers were up against.

"The fact that he knows the terrain very well and has a police radio in the car make the search even more difficult," the staff sergeant admitted.

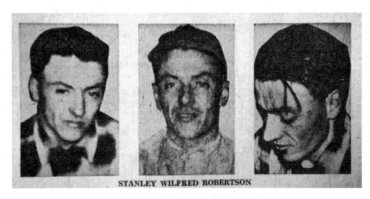

STANLEY WILFRED ROBERTSON

Stanley Robertson, 1970. Reproduced with permission from the *Regina Leader-Post*.

The cruiser and the officers' handguns were found the next day not far from the farm, but Robertson remained elusive. RCMP believed he may even have managed to slip home undetected after the shooting to get a heavier jacket, boots and a .22.

The search started with four tracking dogs, three RCMP airplanes and any officer who could get to the scene quickly, and expanded from there. Within days, the ranks of armed officers rose to about sixty men, three more airplanes were added, and armoured military vehicles were loaned by the Canadian Forces. Roadblocks went up around the province.

Armed police officers searched every car that went through, one officer scrutinizing faces and identification while another stood nearby, armed and ready. "Those who man them mean business," observed one newspaper reporter about the roadblocks.

Officers worked around the clock, chilled to the bone as the fall grew colder, living on coffee and sandwiches prepared by legions of worried women looking for some way to help. A Prince Albert garage worked around the clock putting winter tires on police vehicles, doing whatever repairs were needed to get them back on the punishing roads.

The search was agonizing and dangerous, with everyone already painfully aware of what Robertson might do if he was found.

"We are concerned for further loss of life ...," an RCMP spokesman said. "We fear that if we find the fugitive in one of those clumps of trees and send two of our men in only one will come out."

To protect themselves, officers looking for Robertson wore army helmets and bulletproof vests, and were heavily armed. People who lived in the area stayed inside with their doors locked.

Everyone was jumpy. So when a car crashed through one of the roadblocks, police responded with gravity. As the car approached, an officer fired a shot at one of its tires, sending the vehicle careening around the road and into a roll. There were four teenagers in the car, youths who had escaped from the Saskatchewan Boys' School and were making their break. One of the officers had sent this out over the radio, alerting other officers that it was only kids in the car, that Robertson wasn't among them, but the message wasn't received. A police bullet went through the car door and hit the driver in a leg, before tearing an ugly, internal path toward his heart. The teen, 15-year-old John Muskeg, died at the scene.

And still, there was no sign of Stanley Robertson.

"If I could only find him I would walk up to him and tell him to give himself up," said Robertson's uncle, Abe Wall. "He must have gone out of his head. I don't know. He had a big fight with his wife that day. He never drank and wasn't drinking that day. Something must have happened in his mind."

As the manhunt wore on, police again stepped up their efforts, bringing in another fifty officers from around the province to search for Robertson on the ground. The officers worked in groups, each aided by trained tracking dogs brought from Manitoba and Alberta to sniff out the killer. But even the dogs failed to track the experienced woodsman through the dense bush and bog.

As the days passed, police grew desperate, and made another plea for information—no matter how seemingly insignificant. The RCMP offered a $5,000 reward, and put Robertson's name on the country's Most Wanted list.

But by December, the RCMP started to scale back the search, taking down roadblocks one by one, sending officers home to their detachments, on to other searches, other domestic arguments, other dangerous men.

Winter fell, cold and long, and still a small contingent of officers searched, checking nearly every abandoned farm structure in the three Prairie provinces—every empty building "from the U.S. border north," said one officer—and checking out trails of smoke rising from remote cabins.

It was May when they finally found him. Nearly seven months to the day Robertson fled into the bush, Sergeant W.J. Regetnig and a tracking dog finally hunted him down. It was a few days after the RCMP had stepped up the search again for the spring.

Robertson was sitting on the ground under a large pine tree with a .22 under one arm, a rifle under the other, and an RCMP revolver tucked into his clothes. He had two boxes of shells and a hunting knife, and was less than three miles from his home.

Long before the murders, Stanley Robertson had vowed that if he was ever the subject of a police search, he would not be captured alive. He kept his word.

The gunshot wound in his chest appeared to be self-inflicted, and he looked like he had been dead a long time. Maybe even since the day he killed the two officers.

FOREST RANGER

The Beattys loved Barney Belcourt, and he loved them. Barney came to live with the family in 1917, shortly before Christmas, taking up residence in one of the upstairs bedrooms at the Beattys' small house near Theodore. He became part of the family almost right away.

Ed Beatty especially appreciated that Barney was reliable and honest. Ed had never had a better man working for him, and therefore had no problem recommending Barney for a job as a ranger at the Beaver Hills Forest Reserve, where Ed himself worked as a ranger. Being a forest ranger was a good job with good pay, and after Barney got hired he was always happy to share his money with the family. He was kind and generous—a little too generous, if anything—always giving little presents to Mrs. Beatty, and the couple's four boys. Barney was even kind to the horses.

The boys worshipped Barney, and when he was at home they followed him around all day, always at his heels as he worked around the yard. Mrs. Beatty liked Barney too. She was a pale and sickly woman, plagued by illness much of her life, and he always took special care of her. Barney wouldn't let Mrs. Beatty carry even a billet of wood or a pail of water by herself, and she, in turn, had nothing but praise for him. Barney gave Mrs. Beatty money whenever she asked for it and he often bought her little presents and items for around the house. Once he bought silverware, and, on another occasion, dishes Mrs. Beatty could never have afforded otherwise.

But Barney Belcourt was most generous with the Beattys' daughter, Thelma. She was a happy and spirited girl, and she loved Belcourt and his gifts. Barney loved her, too.

Thelma was only twelve, but Barney always thought she carried on more like a girl of fifteen. She talked just like a grown-up person, he said once, even if she wasn't.

Thelma was so young and beautiful that even though Barney knew it was wrong, he had been doing it anyway, slipping quietly into her room at night when everyone else in the house was asleep.

It was on one such night in September of 1918 that Barney decided he couldn't bear his guilt anymore. Ed Beatty was out of town for the night with one of the boys, and Barney called to Mrs. Beatty from the door of her bedroom. She got up, bleary eyed, and put on her shoes and coat over her nightgown before meeting him in the kitchen. As they sat together in the dark, Barney confessed everything he'd done with the girl. Mrs. Beatty didn't believe him at first. She had asked Thelma about that sort of thing once before, but Thelma had sworn it hadn't happened. The girl had even said she'd take an oath on the Bible to prove she was telling the truth.

"Mother, that child, this Thelma, she just got you blind fooled," Barney told Mrs. Beatty.

Mrs. Beatty called Thelma out of bed and into the kitchen, and asked the girl if what Barney was saying was true. Thelma stood silently for a few minutes before answering.

"Yes," she said finally.

They all stayed quiet for a while longer, then Barney told Thelma to go back to bed. The girl went to her room but she could still hear them talking low in the kitchen, her mother's voice trembling, someone—was it Barney? Mother?—talking about giving her a beating. Then Thelma heard a struggle, a shout, something like a yell, and when she poked her head out the door, her mother was lying still on the floor.

Barney dragged Mrs. Beatty by her coat and pushed her down into the cellar. Then he kneeled on the cellar door and nailed it closed while Mrs. Beatty pushed on it from below. By that time, George, the baby, had awoken and was crying, so Barney took him upstairs and put him in bed with the boys.

Ronald had been sleeping with his little brother Tyrell when he was awakened by a noise from downstairs. The 9-year-old lay still as Barney and Thelma burst into the room, and Barney placed the baby down onto the bed beside him. Ronald heard Thelma crying, begging Barney not to kill their mother.

"Pass me some water quick, I am fainting," Mrs. Beatty was calling from the cellar.

Barney opened the door a bit and passed some water and a towel through to the woman. He could see that she had blood on her face and she was crying, saying, "Oh Barney, let me out. Have you not a heart?"

Barney didn't answer. Instead, he took a sack of his clothes, grabbed a couple of Thelma's dresses and gathered some bread and bacon from the larder. Then he tied up the sack and took Thelma by the hand.

"Shut up," he told her. "And don't scream anymore."

* * *

Ronald lay awake in bed until daylight, then he got up, got dressed and went downstairs. The house was eerily calm. There was nobody downstairs or out in the yard, no one in the barn.

As Ronald came back inside, Tyrell called him over, and the 6-year-old showed Ronald a series of bloody nails that had been tapped into the cellar door. Ronald chiseled the door open and the boys found their mother slumped on the dirt floor of the cellar. Her face was battered on one side, covered in dried blood. When Ronald tried to talk to her, she moved her lips, but no sounds came out. The boys sat down in the kitchen and ate breakfast, then walked half an hour to the neighbour's house for help.

Barney Belcourt had saddled two horses, and he and Thelma rode a few miles before it started to get light. Knowing people would be searching for them soon—and knowing they would be easy to find riding together in the open—Barney chose a hiding spot in a little bluff of poplars, laying his coat on the cold ground to wait out the day. It was chilly that morning, grey and bleak. Barney started a fire, but put it out when he realized people could use the smoke to find them. Lying there in the trees, he did again to Thelma what he had done before.

The girl was distraught and worried about her mother, but Barney prom-

The stairs from the cellar, where the body of Barney Belcourt's victim was found, 1934. Copyright Department of Justice. Reproduced with the permission of the Minister of Public Works and Government Services Canada (2008). Source: Library and Archives Canada/Department of Justice fonds, RG13, B-1, Vol. 1496, file cc 95.

ised her Mrs. Beatty would be okay. She's all right, he assured Thelma, she could open the cellar door with one strong push. But Barney was beginning to worry too. He had planned to take Thelma away and marry her before Mr. Beatty got home, hoping that marriage would save him from his sins—or at least from jail—but he was starting to realize that his plan might not work. Barney was also starting to feel sorry for Thelma, out there in the cold and feeling upset about her mother. He told Thelma to ride back to the farm, and asked her to tell Mrs. Beatty he was sorry for what he had done. He said he was going to Regina to turn himself in to the police, and kissed Thelma one last time before she left.

Mrs. Beatty wasn't looking well when the doctor arrived. Ed Beatty, having been summoned from his boarding house in Yorkton, had picked up the doctor on his way back home, and the two came in to find Mrs. Beatty in bed with some of the men from neighbouring farms and their wives gathered grimly around. Mrs. Beatty's eyes were glazed, her pupils as broad and lifeless as spots of spilled ink; her breath heavy and irregular. She died in bed a short time later, around the same time several parties of men were heading out in search of Barney Belcourt.

It was Ed Beatty himself who found Barney the next day, camped out in those poplars with a rifle on the ground and one of Beatty's horses lying down beside him. Beatty pointed a .22 at his former friend and employee, and Barney walked out of the trees with his hands up.

"I will be good," he was saying. "I will be good."

Ed Beatty fired the rifle once into the air to alert the other teams, while a police officer who had been helping with the search handcuffed Belcourt and charged him with murder. When Barney Belcourt found out that Mrs. Beatty had died, he asked to see her. He said he wanted to see her face one last time.

During his trial in Melville in October of 1918, Barney Belcourt recalled his great love for the woman he killed.

"I liked her very much. I loved her. She was a very nice woman indeed," he testified. "She treated me like my mother ... They treated me good and I treated them good too."

Belcourt said he didn't hit Mrs. Beatty or push her into the cellar, and didn't know she was so badly injured by what he claimed was an accidental fall.

"I would have taken her out of the cellar and attended to her myself ...," he said. "I never want to see Mrs. Beatty hurt for I liked her. She was a good woman."

But his affection for the woman wasn't enough. After a brief deliberation, a jury convicted Belcourt of murder and he was sentenced to hang early in 1919. He took the verdict without

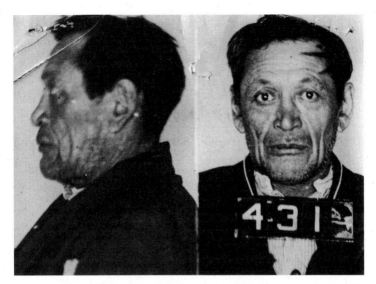

Barney Belcourt, 1934. Copyright Department of Justice. Reproduced with the permission of the Minister of Public Works and Government Services Canada (2008). Source: Library and Archives Canada/Department of Justice fonds, RG13, B-1, Vol. 1496, file cc 95.

emotion, and was taken to the death cell at the Regina jail to await his sentence.

As the date of his execution approached, people began to come forward on Belcourt's behalf and argued that the man's life should be spared. At 38, he had never before had any trouble with the law, and many believed he hadn't intended to hurt Mrs. Beatty. Some familiar with the case maintained Mr. and Mrs. Beatty bore part of the responsibility for the trouble by failing to keep a closer watch on their girl, and many found Thelma's version of events a little bit suspect.

Yorkton lawyer Vincent Reynolds Smith pointed to the fact that Belcourt had asked to see Mrs. Beatty's body as proof of his lack of malice.

"It occurs to us that it is repugnant to human nature that a murderer would care to look upon a person who he had murdered," Smith wrote in a letter to Ottawa on the subject, expressing his strong opinion that Mrs. Beatty's injuries had been accidental.

Prominent Alberta Sheriff Peter Gunn, who had employed Belcourt a few years earlier, described him as having a kind disposition, free from cruelty—though Gunn noted there was a strain of insanity running through Belcourt's family. Still, Gunn said Belcourt was a reliable workman, whose reputation was "above reproach in every way."

Another high-ranking Alberta official, provincial secretary Jean Leon Cote, echoed Gunn's sentiments, saying there was "an entire absence of any evil or vicious traits" in Belcourt's character. Even the judge who heard Belcourt's trial didn't believe Belcourt had intended to hurt the woman.

The arguments were persuasive, and only weeks before he was to be hanged, Barney Belcourt had his sentence commuted to life imprisonment. He was transferred to the Saskatchewan Penitentiary in Prince Albert to begin his sentence. He remained there until 1928, when he was granted a ticket of leave after serving ten years of his life sentence.

The warden recommended Belcourt's release, saying he believed that confinement had had a positive effect on Belcourt, and that Belcourt would lead an honest life in the community.

But Barney Belcourt came out of prison a much different man. He now spent his time drifting from town to town, sometimes working, but more often fighting and drinking beer. Friends noticed him talking to himself sometimes, and soon his behaviour became increasingly odd and confused. He seemed to be losing his memory, and he was irritable and easily angered.

He was finally re-arrested in 1934 and transferred to the Provincial Mental Hospital in North Battleford. He died there six years later.

MIDDLE-AGED CROOKS

As he sat in the interrogation room, Calvin Getz gave some serious thought to his situation. He was in big trouble, that much he knew for certain. He was looking at years in prison, and he could imagine exactly what it was like in there—no booze, no sex, the other inmates doing whatever they pleased. And for what? He didn't even get his share of the money. Getz didn't need to think long before he decided what he was going to do.

He told the police everything.

* * *

Calvin Getz met Royal John Derry in January of 1974. Derry was several years older than Getz, and impressed Getz with his smooth manner, and his taste for nice cars and other luxuries. The two men hit it off right away, and Derry seemed to be especially fond of his new young friend.

"You are like my lost son whom I found again," Derry told him once.

Derry often went to Getz's ranch near Craven. He seemed to like it out there, and was always interested in the work Getz was doing with his Arabian horses. He was also very interested in Getz's job at Brink's.

Getz started working as a guard at Brink's in 1968. He became a driver for the armoured truck company, and was later promoted to messenger. Being messenger was a step up for Getz; the messenger was in charge of the truck and the money, and always rode in back with the valuable load.

As the men's friendship progressed through the winter and spring of 1974, Derry would regularly stop by the Brink's office in Regina to visit Getz. It was against the company's rules to have a member of the public at the office, but no one seemed to mind. The same men had worked together for a long time, and they sometimes bent the rules for each other. Security wasn't as tight as it had once been—a fact not lost on Roy Derry.

Derry talked Getz into the scheme slowly, over the course of months. Derry was a good friend to Getz, and a lot of what he said eventually started to make sense. Derry told Getz everyone was corrupt, that the whole world was crooked. Why should they be any different? On top of that, Getz had debts to pay. He had divorced recently, and his financial problems weighed heavily enough to make Derry's arguments appealing.

So Getz, Derry, and Derry's friend, Donald Ziegler, started putting together a plan for a heist.

Things finally came together in the first week of August 1974, and the three men held a rehearsal to see how things would work. The plan hit an unfortunate snag when Ziegler happened to bump into a senior police officer in the doorway of the government office building where the heist was to take place.

Police Superintendent Joseph Juno was irritated when a man brushed rudely by him, and he immediately recognized Ziegler from past investigations. The keen-eyed officer also noticed Ziegler had a bag folded under his arm, and noted there was a Brink's truck idling outside. But the run-in with Juno didn't derail the plan. The three men assumed the officer probably hadn't even noticed Ziegler—or at least hadn't recognized him. So, with the rehearsal completed, the men were ready for the real thing.

It started at about 1 p.m. on August 9. Getz was working that day, riding in the back of the armoured truck as it picked up a shipment of money from the main branch of the Bank of Nova Scotia in downtown Regina. The load was fifteen bags filled with money, $141,000, which was to be mailed to credit unions in fifteen towns around the province later that day.

As the driver headed to the next pick-up at a government office building on Albert Street and Hill Avenue, Getz got to work. From his spot in the back of the armoured truck, he took the postal tags off six money bags and loaded the bags into one bigger bag.

When they arrived at their stop, Getz took the big bag into the building. He was supposed to fill it with deposits, but instead he went to the third floor and into the bathroom where Ziegler was waiting. The men got into adjoining cubicles. Getz passed the six white canvas bags full of money under the divider to Ziegler, and Ziegler passed back six similar-looking bags he and Derry had fashioned. Those bags were full of bundles of white paper and weighted with pieces of lead. Getz left the bathroom with the dummy bags and picked up his deposits around the building as usual. Ziegler took off with the bags of money.

The rest of the Brink's run was uneventful, with fifteen bags—including the phonies—delivered to the city's main post office at about five that evening, just a little later than usual.

Getz was at home when Derry called him and told him the haul was about $60,000. The money was supposed to be divvied up equally three ways, and when Derry offered to look after Getz's share, Getz agreed to let him keep it for a while. Getz didn't know what to do with all that cash anyway. Derry, meanwhile, had plenty of ideas. In the next few days, he burned through at least $16,000—buying a swank mink coat, a couple thousand dollars worth of tools, a new barbecue and ordering new glass for the windows of his house. He also paid off thousands of dollars owing on his mortgage, income tax and other debts. He paid for everything in cash, usually small denominations. Several people who dealt with Derry noticed the money he gave them was damp. But Derry wouldn't be flush for long.

Three days after the robbery, a swarm of police officers descended on Derry's house, tearing the home apart looking for money, white paper, lead, and any other evidence that could connect him to the robbery. All the police found of interest was a large number of jewellery tags and a collection of high-quality imitation diamonds. Officers who searched Ziegler's house had a bit more luck, turning up three white canvas money bags full of coins and a business card with Derry's name and phone number on it.

With the evidence of a few eyewitnesses at the scene—and with the information from Superintendent Juno—it was all the police needed. Derry, Ziegler and Getz were arrested and charged with robbery.

A few days later, a cleaning woman at a downtown department store found a water-soaked plastic bag containing nearly $4,000 in torn bills shoved in a garbage bin in the women's bathroom. A few $20 bills had also been discovered earlier in a coffee shop garbage can, but the rest of the stolen money was never found.

* * *

Calvin Getz took the witness stand at Court of Queen's Bench in June of 1975. He had already pleaded guilty to theft and was facing two years in jail for his part in the Brinks caper.

Now, the inside man was to play a key role in the case against Derry and Ziegler.

Getz's testimony came with some peril; he was mysteriously dosed with hallucinogenic drugs that were slipped into a drink shortly before the trial, and had to be treated in hospital. A missing preliminary hearing transcript—the only thing stolen in a courthouse break-in—delayed matters further, but eventually the trial proceeded with Getz testifying against his two former friends.

"I wasn't prepared to do five years," he told court. "The two fellows had all the money while I had nothing and I knew they won't do anything for me."

The jury found Derry and Ziegler guilty as charged.

As the trial closed, Justice Sandy MacPherson expressed his own opinions about the heist, describing it as well-planned with "the touch of professionals about it."

"Things went wrong, and the things that went wrong ... were your own errors, and they were very stupid errors," MacPherson told the men. "They prove that you're not as clever as you think you are."

MacPherson said the men made an especially serious mistake when they

Sketch of Roy Derry, 1990. Artist Gail Duesterbeck. Reproduced with permission from the *Regina Leader-Post*.

picked Getz as an accomplice, describing Getz as "the classic nice guy who loses ball games" and "a fellow who couldn't be a crook for very long."

"You picked the wrong man," he told them. "Getz just was not the criminal type. As soon as you picked him you were bound to lose."

As MacPherson continued, he spoke specifically to Derry, expounding on Derry's "colossal errors" during the heist and afterward.

"All that money you spent was dreadful," MacPherson told him. "It wasn't very smart."

At that point Derry could not take it any more. Jumping from his seat, Derry told the judge he could make as much as $20,000 in a single week selling diamonds

"I can produce $15,000 to $20,000 clean money ...," Derry said, his voice rising to almost a yell. "It's clean money, it has no ties with Brink's."

Derry added that the clean money might actually still be damp, because he liked to keep currency hidden in various places, including underground. Then Derry stopped talking—possibly swayed by the idea of having to pay back the missing Brink's money. After conferring with his lawyer, Derry decided not to say anything more about his earning potential.

While MacPherson admitted he found both the caper and the trial "amusing," the sentence he handed down to Derry and Ziegler wasn't. He sentenced both men to seven years in prison, telling them: "The public deserves to be protected from you for a long time."

"You are just a couple of middle-aged crooks ...," MacPherson said. "I really doubt if you will ever change."

* * *

The Brink's job wasn't the beginning—or the end—for Roy Derry.

Raised in Kenora, Ontario, Derry quit school in Grade 3. He was hired by the CPR when he was about 14, but left that position during the Second World War and started drifting around the country.

Derry's criminal career started in 1946, when he was just a teenager, with a $20 fine for unlawful purchase of a weapon. Convictions for property and nuisance crimes followed with frequency in the years that followed.

Released from prison after the Brink's robbery, Derry was soon convicted of sexual assault for drugging a woman in his apartment, shaving her pubic hair, writing on her with magic marker and giving her hickies around her body. He was sentenced to three years in prison for the bizarre assault, and committed another, similar offence just weeks after his release.

In one of the cases, Derry tried to blackmail his victim by telling her he would show sexually explicit photos of her to her friends and family. He also forged a letter from a doctor saying the woman had a disease which could only be treated by having sex with him.

"Mr. Derry is an ultimate user of people. He is pathological in that respect. He is a con man," Crown prosecutor John Stoesser said during one of Derry's many court proceedings.

Stoesser also called Derry "a life criminal, and proud of it."

A prison psychologist found Derry had a "moral disability," and showed little concern, empathy or compassion for those he had victimized throughout his life.

During one of his bail hearings, Derry boasted he still had the money from the Brink's robbery, and promised to turn it over to the police if he was granted bail. The judge didn't take the deal.

In 1989, Derry pleaded guilty to fraud for selling $2 worth of brass filings to a Regina woman for hundreds of dollars, telling her it was gold dust. It was just one of his many scams.

"Actually we've always been quite surprised he's managed to do all the things he has and stayed alive," noted Norm Marchinko, the police officer in charge of the Regina Major Crimes section at the time.

One lawyer who represented Derry described him as an interesting character, "a Damon Runyon type," with a good sense of humour and likeable qualities.

Others were not so kind.

In 1990, when the 61-year-old Derry was sentenced to six years in prison for scamming a convenience store clerk out of $42,500 in a cigarette scheme, Deputy Police Chief Ed Swayze was less than sentimental about Derry's long criminal career.

"I made up my mind a long time ago never to waste my personal time or the department's time to talk about people like Royal Derry," Swayze said. "He is the most despicable human being in Regina."

THE KILLING ROOM

Killing is messy business. It's not only the killing, either, it's everything that comes along with it; the noise and the smell and the blood. There is always so much blood.

Ronald Lischynski was standing in the killing room with the smell of it all around when he told Kevin Melnychuk what he wanted to do. Kevin had worked at the Yorkton Abattoir a couple years earlier, and had recently been hired back. He wasn't always a great employee—sometimes late and unreliable, and rough with the equipment—but when he came back to Ron asking for a job, Ron said he could probably use him on the kill floor. Ron said he could maybe use Kevin for something else, too, but they could talk about that later.

Later became a day in the fall of 1985, as the two stood together in the killing room. Ron told Kevin he wanted his wife, Darlene, "put away." *Killed.*

Kevin laughed it off at first, but Ron brought it up again later. He said they'd been having problems at home and at work. Darlene thought he was having an affair and she was threatening to leave him. Something had to be done. Ron said he'd worked too long and too hard to get what he had, he wasn't going to lose half of it to Darlene.

At first Ron thought maybe Kevin could shoot Darlene out on the farm. During deer season, you know, make it look like some kind of hunting accident. But when deer season came and went without any such accidents, Ron came up with other plans. Drugs could work, but it would be risky because insurance doesn't cover suicide. Then he thought of the meat saw with the broken switch. He said he'd pay $10,000. Maybe as much as $20,000.

* * *

Even before Ron started to plot his wife's murder, things hadn't been going very well for the Yorkton couple. Darlene was becoming increasingly worried about her husband. It had started in the summer; Ron was tense, not sleeping, flying off the handle at things that never would have bothered him before. At other times, Ron was depressed, crying, talking of suicide. Darlene found a suicide note once, but tore it up before all the horrible words it contained could become real. Ron was taking pills and drinking a lot, which didn't help. Darlene thought Ron seemed to be walking around in a daze, and there were periods of time he didn't appear to remember at all. Like that time with the combine. Ron didn't believe Darlene when she told him he'd already fixed it, and he had to go outside and look at the weld to prove it to himself.

Sometimes he would lose his balance, and his face often looked flushed and odd. Once, when they stopped to visit some friends, Ron slumped down on the couch in his parka and fell asleep. He looked almost like a zombie at times. Not like himself at all.

Other people noticed, too. Salesman Glen deVries started to notice in the fall, and as the winter chill settled in Ron's behaviour seemed to be getting progressively worse. When Glen saw Ron at the abattoir on the morning of February 10, Ron chewed him out in front of everybody, yelling at him so loudly that the employees stopped to stare.

"You'd think he was asleep, but he wasn't," Glen said later. "He was walking around doing things, he just wasn't himself. There was no humour."

After the confrontation with Glen, Ron left work and drove to a Yorkton motel to meet Kevin and Kevin's pal, Mike. Sitting around in a room, the three men chatted for a while, drinking a couple beers together, and talking about the finer points of killing.

"A meat cutter is a tradesman. But a butcher, there's a big difference. A butcher is someone that kills ...," Kevin said.

Mike hadn't appreciated that meat cutting was such a skill.

"You mean you can go to a tech school and take meat cutting?" he asked.

"Yeah," Ron said.

"I didn't know that," said Mike.

"Oh yeah," Kevin said. "Not butchering. Butchering is killing."

"Well," Mike said. "Anybody can kill."

Kevin couldn't. He was too scared to do it. He started shaking every time he even thought of doing what Ron had asked him to do. That's why Kevin called Mike. Mike had killed before, did some broad with an ice pick, and he was looking to make some fast money to head down east. Mike could do the job.

"I can waste her anytime you say ...," Mike told Ron. "You tell me and I'll do it."

Ron said he didn't want there to be any suffering, and suggested electrocution might work best. He said Mike could go to the couple's other business, Lakeroad Meats, in the morning, when Darlene would be working there alone.

"She'd come and serve you. From there on it's your baby. There's power, like 220 volts. It would make it an accident, like, big electrocution, but it's accidental. It's much easier than shooting or anything else."

"It's gotta be an accident," Mike agreed.

"That's the easiest thing," said Ron.

Ron said he could make sure the back door was open, maybe give Mike a key, or Mike could go in through the corrals. He thought $17,000 sounded fair.

The two men discussed how the problem with the grinder switch could work to their advantage.

"Remove the ground wire. Get one 'a the hot lines, put it to the frame ... What's on the ground there, is it concrete?" Mike asked.

"Concrete," Ron confirmed.

"Okay, it could be wet. That would be cool."

Ron gave Mike directions, then went to the car to get a pen and drew a little map. He said he would have to go home to get a picture of Darlene and a bit of money.

"Are you really committed? Are you really committed to wasting her?" Mike asked. "To me doing it? Are you committed to it?"

"Long time ago," Ron said.

Ron had just gone back to work after his meeting with Mike when Darlene showed up at the abattoir with a load of sausage. She thought her husband seemed worse than ever. He hadn't even brushed his hair that morning, and when they went for lunch, he barely touched his food, pushing the liver and onions around on his plate with little interest. He told her he had to go back home after lunch to pick up something for the abattoir.

Ron showed up back at Mike's hotel room around three that afternoon with a picture of Darlene and $400 in cash. The picture was from his parents' anniversary party. She looked pretty much the same, maybe her hair was a bit shorter now, but that was about it.

Ron and Mike worked out the money details, and the deal was done.

Then the cops barged in and arrested Ron for trying to hire someone to kill his wife. Mike Morrissey was an undercover RCMP officer, and their entire exchange had been caught on tape.

Ron spent a couple of months at a psychiatric hospital before he was released on bail.

When he got out, he moved back in with Darlene and their daughters. They wanted him there, and Darlene said she had no fear of her husband.

"He wasn't his usual self all that fall, and I just wasn't scared because that wasn't his usual self," she said.

Neighbours, friends and the family's minister were completely shocked by the allegation that Ron had tried to have his wife killed. For many, it was unbelievable.

At his trial, Ron testified he didn't remember the months leading up to his meeting with Mike. He agreed that it was his voice caught on tape planning Darlene's murder, though Ron thought it still didn't really sound like him.

A doctor who examined Ron found him to be "a fairly normal individual," though he couldn't say conclusively whether Ron was telling the truth about his amnesiac episodes.

Even Ron's lawyer couldn't make sense of what had happened, calling it "a paradoxical situation and hard to understand."

"This man, in whatever his state of mind, [came] to some sort of conclusion as to what the solution was to his problems," Aaron Fox said. "Obviously a very wrong solution and a very serious offence, but I don't think there is any question ... that his thinking was not completely rational and was being influenced by other sources."

At the trial, Darlene again pledged her support for the man who had planned to kill her.

"I never planned to leave him even when this happened," she said. "I felt he needed me more."

After listening to the facts of the case, Justice Joseph McIntyre said he, too, was unable to make sense of the crime.

"The factor that I find so very unusual is that you and your wife were living together at the time, apparently on the face of it by what we're told getting along well, and yet you deliberately arranged or tried to arrange for her death by drugs, electrocution or shooting," he said.

A jury found Ronald Lischynski guilty of counselling to murder his wife, and he was later sentenced to four years in prison. After hearing the sentence, Darlene wept and embraced her husband tightly before he was taken into custody by RCMP officers in court. Ron showed little reaction, almost like he was in a daze.

STRONGER THAN DEATH

The house has been burning for more than seven hours, and it is burning still. Whenever the fire starts to rage, the fire-fighters move in, bring down the flames, then retreat until the house flares up again. They repeat this routine over and over as night turns to dawn, and continue as dawn finally gives way to morning.

The specially trained officers from the police tactical team are poised around the house in north central Regina. They are invisible but everywhere, their sights set, each one of them ready to fire at any moment. The suspect is violent, possibly armed. There is almost nothing left of the rundown little house by then—just the charred outer walls, and everything else reduced to ash and rubble. And it's still burning.

The man they want has been in the house all night long, and they haven't heard from him in a while. The police nego-tiator is still trying to make contact. Up until now, they would sometimes see his dark shadow through the windows, passing through the house like a ghost. At one point, he was even yelling at them, screaming "come and get me" and throwing a TV out the window toward them. Now he's quiet, and everyone is thinking he's got to be dead.

But when the police finally throw canisters of tear gas into the smouldering wreckage around nine that morning, David Alexson comes stumbling out with his hands up.

He's looking pretty bad, but he's alive. And he's under arrest for murder.

Alexson needs to see a doctor, so he is taken to the Pasqua Hospital. He inhaled a lot of smoke while he was inside the burning house, at first pacing around looking for a way out, and later curled inside a refrigerator to escape the smoke and flames. The 33-year-old is thoroughly examined and X-rayed, and appears to be fine when he is given a chance to meet with his lawyer alone. He talks to his lawyer for a few minutes in a hospital room, then steps out into the hallway to get some water. Then he's gone.

Just hours after the fiery standoff, the police are after Alexson once more. Officers mobilize quickly for the hunt, and everyone is relieved when a police dog sniffs him out before too long, finding him hiding under a trailer in a parking lot at the exhibition grounds, just a couple of blocks away from the hospital. Alexson is arrested again. This time he's taken straight to the police station.

Detective-Sergeant Rod Buckingham sits down with Alexson in an interrogation room at the police station in Regina later that day. It's Mother's Day, 2003. Alexson is wearing a hospital gown and he's coughing and wheezing, distraught and agitated. He wants to talk to his wife, to wish her a happy Mother's Day and tell her he loves her. Buckingham lets him make the call.

But Buckingham wants something too. He wants Alexson to help a different mother, a mother Alexson has never met, by telling the police what he did with her son's body. You can give her back her son, Buckingham tells him. Alexson isn't talking. His lawyer told him not to say anything, so after listening to Buckingham for a while he asks to go back to his cell.

* * *

At the beginning, the police didn't know exactly what had happened, but they knew it was bad.

They found the crime scene after a woman named Roxy called to report a break-in. It was a fairly routine call at first, but an officer who talked to Roxy outside the house soon realized something more serious had occurred.

"I'm not going in there," Roxy told him. "There's blood everywhere."

It was a gruesome scene. Bloody handprints on the wall, blood spots on the ceiling and walls, blood soaked into the cellar stairs. There was no body, but so much blood.

* * *

Before long, Alexson asks to talk to Buckingham again. This time, he says he'll tell the police everything.

"The whole fucking enchilada right now on a silver platter," he promises. He just wants to make it clear that some other people who were around that day didn't take part in the murder. Doesn't want anyone else going down for something he did.

He's obviously feeling better, sharper. His eyes are darting around the room, staring into the camera mounted by the ceiling in the interrogation room. He's in a much better mood, too, even laughing as he remembers the scene at the hospital.

"The other day when I tried to fuck off from the hospital, shit, I guess that musta kinda freaked you guys out a bit, eh?" he asks Buckingham with a laugh.

"You betcha," Buckingham says.

"'Son of a bitch,' you musta been thinking, 'This guy fucked off,'" Alexson chuckles. "After all that, taking off again. Couldn't believe you guys took off the handcuffs and shackles."

"We can't either," says Buckingham.

Then Alexson tells Buckingham the story.

* * *

Tim Schick was 38 and had been working as a business consultant in Regina, having recently moved back to Saskatchewan with his wife. Schick was at work on May 7, but instead of going home, he decided to go for a beer at a place in the north end. He was sitting alone at the bar when an old friend from school came in, and Schick joined the guy and his group at a table. They spent the evening catching up, joking around, and talking about the NHL playoffs.

Schick left the bar around 12:30, saying he was heading home. He was driving around 6th Avenue and Retallack Street when he stopped to talk to a couple of girls, and they got into his car. The three went to pick up some beer, then headed to a house just a few blocks away.

"Is this where I get killed?" Schick joked as they pulled up.

Two men, Gary Sparvier and David Alexson, were already at the house when Schick and the girls arrived, and they all sat around for a bit drinking and talking. The group went out later and Schick bought more beer, then the five went to Roxy's place on Angus Street.

It was there that things went bad. It happened fast. Alexson wanted Schick's money, demanded Schick's bank card, his PIN. When Schick wouldn't give it up, the two men started tussling on the floor. Alexson drew a knife.

The girls ran out of the house. Sparvier took off. Alexson and Schick were alone.

After that, it was a blur of blood and violence. Schick kneeling on the floor, Alexson binding his hands with a phone cord ripped from the wall. Schick in the cellar, injured and begging, Alexson in the kitchen thinking about what to do next. Schick hiding in the back bedroom. The hammer.

"I wanted to let him go, you know?" Alexson tells Buckingham during a walk-through of the crime scene. Handcuffed and shackled, Alexson leads Buckingham through the vicious crime step by step. He points to the spot where Schick finally crumpled to the livingroom floor.

"I was telling him, 'I'm going to let you go alright?'" he says. "But he was already gone. He was already slipping away."

Alexson loaded Schick's body into the trunk of Schick's car and drove out of town, stripping the body nude and dumping it in the water at the edge of Pasqua Lake, on a reserve just northeast of Regina. The body was only half-submerged in the water, and Alexson tried to push it down a bit by placing a rock on the abdomen.

David Alexson, June 10, 2004, photographer Roy Antal, courtesy *Regina Leader-Post*.

After his confession, Alexson says he will take the police to the body. The first trip is a bust, with Alexson unable —or unwilling—to find the spot. But on the second trip, Alexson leads the police directly to it.

"Go right down to the waterline ... He's right there," Alexson says, as the car pulls toward the edge of the lake. "Fuck, they're going to be shocked, man, when they see him."

The body was in such bad shape police investigators advised Schick's family not to look at it. Schick had been stabbed at least twenty-nine times. His throat had been slashed and his skull was fractured. The pathologist concluded Schick could have died from almost any of his injuries.

A family spokesperson described Tim Schick as a dedicated son, a loving husband, a kind brother and a good friend.

"He was very outgoing, always had a smile, never hurt anybody intentionally," he said. "He was just a nice person."

* * *

A little more than two months later, the police are looking for David Alexson again.

This time, he has escaped from the Regina jail, where he was awaiting trial for Schick's murder.

Alexson had obviously been working on his escape for a while, digging a hole through the shower wall in the ancient jail building, steadily working his way through the crumbling structure. He had patched the hole with pieces of chewed-up Styrofoam to keep anyone from noticing it.

On the night of July 31, Alexson and an 18-year-old accomplice broke through the wall, squeezing through the small hole, then scaling down the wall of the jail using small pieces of rope tied together. The men climbed two fences, got into a waiting car and were gone. The teenager was arrested the next day, but police continue to look for Alexson, knowing fully the terrible violence of which he is capable.

A week later, a man in a cabin community an hour east of Regina finds Alexson sleeping in a trailer. The man calls the police, and he and other cottagers watch the trailer while they wait for officers to arrive. When Alexson comes outside they surround him, drawing in close to make sure there is no chance of him getting away again.

* * *

Security was tight at Court of Queen's Bench in Regina on September 1, 2005. No one was taking any chances with David Alexson.

It was a familiar scene. Alexson had been brought to court on several occasions in anticipation of a plea, but he always changed his mind at the last minute and the deal fell through.

This time, things went as planned. Alexson pleaded guilty to murder, arson, escape from police, escape from jail, break and enter, and assaulting a police officer. Unlike other court appearances—which sometimes involved violent outbursts, including a threat to stab a senior Crown prosecutor—Alexson was sedate and calm. He was dressed entirely in white.

According to the terms of the plea bargain, Alexson would get life in prison with no chance of parole for at least twenty years. He said nothing, just nodded silently as the sentence was passed down.

"The death of Mr. Schick was, to say the least, a brutal and callous taking of a valuable human life," said Justice Ian McLellan, after listening to the facts of the grisly murder. McLellan reminded Alexson that he wouldn't even necessarily get parole in twenty years—only that he would be eligible to apply.

Schick's wife, Tanya, sat quietly in the courtroom listening to the details of her husband's horrific death. Toward the end of the proceedings, the prosecutor read aloud a statement Tanya had written to her husband's killer.

In the statement, Tanya described Tim Schick as a gentle, articulate man who was always there for his family, and she recalled the pain created by his sudden disappearance. She said when Alexson took her husband, he took her own life as she knew it as well. But she vowed he would take nothing more.

"Love is stronger than death, even though it cannot stop death from happening," she wrote. "In the end, life is stronger than death."

A MODEL PRISONER

You asked not to be born, no more did I,
And if we had our Wish, we would not die.
That leaves us, then, but One Sweet Hour of Life,
Since once again this Way we'll not pass by.
—Frank Wesley Anderson, 1942

The Moosomin jail was an imposing building, a sombre fortress of brick and steel rising up from the prairie two miles out of town. The jail was built in 1908 to house the overflow of inmates from the Regina Jail, and in 1928 became a facility for juvenile delinquents. The cells were small and claustrophobic, each five feet wide and a little over eight feet long. The jail's young inmates spent most of their time inside the cramped cells, prohibited even from talking.

Wesley Freeman Anderson was 16 when he got to the jail, a tall and lanky boy with sharp eyes and a sly smile. It was June 21, 1936.

It wasn't the boy's first time in confinement. Anderson was parentless and had already spent much of his life moving between reform schools, detention centres and foster homes. Most recently he'd been at the Portage Reform School, facing a two-year term for a break-in committed in a fit of lovesickness.

"I will admit it was puppy love," Anderson said later. "But you can't trifle with any love."

Anderson had taken a girl to a picture show in Brandon. He was so smitten that when the girl's mother interfered in the relationship, Anderson decided he no longer cared about anything. He broke into a house and stole a dollar, and was promptly sent to the Portage Reform School for two years. He took off from the school a few weeks later, but wasn't free for long. He was caught stealing a bike and two plastic jars of bubble gum from a railroad boxcar in Lanigan. That time, he was sentenced to a year in jail.

The Moosomin jail was something different for Anderson. Though it housed only young men from 16 to 21, it was not an easy place for its prisoners. This was not a school or a reformatory like the other places Anderson had lived—this was a jail, and Anderson was prisoner #Y-3126.

Anderson was given the standard jail-issue prisoner's uniform: coat, pants, shirt, all in the same drab khaki. He was led past the offices and through the yard to Cell 5 in Corridor B, right next to Robert McGrath, a new 15-year-old inmate from Edmonton. Anderson's cell looked like all the others. A bed, a wash basin, a toilet and a bench. And the bars. Those heavy steel bars.

Despite his predicament, Anderson seemed surprisingly happy at the Moosomin Jail. He got along well there, and he often seemed almost carefree, friendly and laughing, causing no trouble for anyone. The guards thought he was a model prisoner.

Anderson was smart and likeable, and he soon earned himself a position in the kitchen, one of a small group of prisoners tasked with cooking for all the other inmates. He was working there as head cook that Sunday, a beautiful August evening. There were four of them working that night and they made vegetable soup with potatoes, like they did every Sunday.

Anderson had talked about breaking out before. Sometimes he and McGrath would whisper between their cells, talking about how the escape would unfold. The plan went like this: Anderson was going to knock out two guards. Then he'd get McGrath, and the two would go outside and steal a car. McGrath knew how to drive, so the two would hit the road.

Supper was at five that night, as always, and Anderson had just finished cleaning up the kitchen when he walked by McGrath's cell. McGrath asked Anderson when he was going to try and get out.

"Right now," Anderson said.

He was armed with a large wooden potato masher.

John Sangster was working the evening shift, three to eleven. It was a quiet night with the usual duties, supervising the cooks in the kitchen, watching the inmates when they got their food, waiting while the inmates prepared the kitchen for the next morning's breakfast, then escorting the cooks back to their cells for the night. That's what Sangster was doing when Anderson hit him in the head. He hit him once, then again. Maybe more. Sangster fell to the floor, and Anderson fished around in the guard's pocket for the keys, then opened McGrath's cell.

"Come on, McGrath, let's go," he said.

Sangster lay on the floor, stunned and bleeding. He tried once to get up but couldn't. When he tried a second time, his hat fell off, and he pulled it back on in a daze. Then he slid slowly down to the floor and fell over, gasping and kicking a little before he went still. Edwin Beard, the other guard on shift, approached Anderson, and Anderson hit him wildly with the masher, then threw the heavy implement at him. Anderson pulled a heavy gate closed between them, locking Beard in the jail's square.

"Don't do it boys, you will never get away with it," Beard said. "You have gone far enough. You will swing for what you have already done."

Beard told the boys to give him the keys, but McGrath wasn't going to make that decision.

"He's the boss, ask him," he said, indicating Anderson.

Anderson looked at Sangster lying on the floor, blood seeping out of his head, staining his dark blue uniform. Anderson ordered McGrath to get some water, and when McGrath returned they knelt together on the concrete floor, sprinkling and splashing water onto the fallen guard, trying to wake him. When that didn't work, Anderson removed the guard's coat and put it under the man's head.

The warden was at home when he got the call. Colonel Allen Sharp had been running the jail since it re-opened eight years earlier, and he had never gotten a call like that before. There had been a handful of escapes, but the prisoners were always caught and brought back quickly. Sharp lived right next to the jail, and was there within a minute or two of receiving the call.

Dr. Edwin J. Ferg arrived a short time later. The warden greeted the doctor at the door, and as they hustled into the jail, he told the doctor that one of his men had been attacked and hurt. Ferg had known the injured guard for several years, and he knew right away it didn't look good for his friend. Sangster was lying just outside the gate to Corridor B, unconscious and wet with water. The 50-year-old guard was at the centre of a growing pool of blood, and was bleeding out of his head, nostrils and mouth.

Dr. Ferg dressed the wounds before taking the guard to the hospital in Moosomin. An x-ray showed the fractures— five bloody, star-shaped breaks in the man's skull. Ferg packed cotton into the wounds and surrounded Sangster with hot water bottles in his hospital bed. Sangster was dead by nightfall.

Anderson went on trial for murder in October. He began the trial as Wesley Freeman Anderson, but during the proceedings a birth certificate was produced showing his name was actually Frank Wesley Anderson.

Anderson's lawyer argued that Anderson hadn't meant to kill the guard, and said his actions could be attributed to the "excitement in the mind of a boy of 16." He pointed out that Anderson had tried to help the guard when he realized the extent of the man's injuries.

"There was no intention to kill Sangster," the lawyer said. "If he had had that intention he would never have done what he did later, give all the assistance he could."

But prosecutors D.H. Towill and W.M. Graham argued Anderson had a plan to escape, and armed himself with a terrible and effective weapon in order to carry out that plan.

After three days of evidence, the jury deliberated little more than an hour before finding Anderson guilty of murder. He was sentenced to hang early in 1937. Justice G.E. Taylor told Anderson there was plenty of evidence to support the jury's verdict, and he gave the teen little hope of clemency.

"It is my duty to convict you and the sentence of this court is that you be confined from this date in the common jail at Regina until January 8, 1937," Justice Taylor said. "On that date you will be hanged by the neck until you are dead, and may God have mercy on your soul."

For the first time during his trial, Anderson was overcome with emotion. He leaned onto a banister and cried like a boy.

* * *

The outcry began almost immediately. It started in North Battleford, "a spontaneous outburst of indignation" is what the papers called it, and it spread quickly. Soon citizens around the country were demanding leniency on the basis of Anderson's age, his troubled childhood, and society's failure to nurture him.

"We believe that it is not a question of this boy's being a menace to society," read a Toronto petition, "but of Society's having been a menace to him."

At 16, Anderson was the youngest person ever to be slated for execution in Canada. In England, the minimum age was 18. A coalition of all the community organizations in North Battleford unanimously passed a resolution that Anderson should be sent to a reform school for the care, treatment and education of juvenile offenders. Groups including the Art Appreciation Club of Saskatoon and the Westminster Church demanded commutation of the death sentence.

On the editorial pages, newspapers demanded leniency. From the pulpit, preachers asked for compassion. Thousands of people signed petitions and sent them to Ottawa, and letters poured in to the Ministry of Justice.

"It seems so unjust that a mere child should be hung," Victoria Tardiff wrote from Parkland, Alberta.

Mrs. James Williamson called Anderson "a misguided child," who had been failed by those around him.

"While recognizing the extreme gravity of his crime, one feels that so young a boy must himself be the victim of environment, training and circumstances," Williamson wrote.

Frank Anderson, 1936. Reproduced with permission from the *Regina Leader-Post*.

In far-off Painsville, Ohio, Mrs. Clarence Holly was so moved by Anderson's plight that she said she yearned to rock him in her arms, to be to him the mother he never had.

"He is only a little boy, the age of some of my own," she wrote. "He is almost a baby, with not even a mother or a father."

At a meeting to discuss wheat marketing policies, five hundred Saskatchewan farmers approved a resolution asking that the teen killer's life be spared. A young Weyburn politician named Tommy Douglas spoke on Anderson's behalf at that meeting, saying no civilized country would execute a boy so young. Douglas argued that had the guard been "more robust," he would have survived Anderson's attack.

In the months following the boy's conviction, support continued to swell.

"Surely at his age the 'kinks' in his character which caused him to commit such a crime could be directed into useful channels making him an honest man some day," wrote Mrs. Marjorie Walker.

On December11, 1936, a reverend at the Regina jail woke up Anderson from an after-dinner nap to tell him the good news. It took a moment for the sleepy teenager to fully understand that he had been granted a reprieve. He would get life instead of death.

Anderson rubbed his eyes and remained silent for several minutes.

"I'm glad," he said finally.

Frank Anderson was moved out of the death cell at Regina Jail, and taken to the Prince Albert Penitentiary to begin serving a life sentence for murder. He wanted to correspond with a guard he'd gotten to know while on death watch in Regina— the two had talked at length about atheism, Darwinism and poetry—but the warden in Prince Albert would not permit the correspondence. Anderson's sisters wrote to him, however, and in time a good relationship developed.

Anderson completed Grades 9, 10, 11 and 12 in prison. After that, the University of Saskatchewan made special arrangements for Anderson to take courses. It was the first time in Canada a prisoner was able to take university classes behind bars.

Prison authorities said Anderson was well-behaved and devoted himself to his studies with tenacity and persistence, "disregarding less worthy ways of occupying his time."

He studied philosophy, and prison staff soon acknowledged that he had moved past the point where they could be of use to him in his education.

When not engaged in his studies, Anderson was the star performer in the prison's gymnastic shows, and penned poetry. In the summer of 1942, he finished "Some Experiments in Rhythm," a little collection of his poems, each perfectly typewritten and neatly bound in crisp cardboard.

A year later, the warden recommended that Anderson be released to serve as a soldier in the Infantry of General Service.

The warden said he believed the structure and control of army life would keep the young lad on a close tether. But in a report on the issue of Anderson's release, Judge Taylor made it clear he had disliked the boy from the start—and was particularly unimpressed with his poetry.

"There is something wrong with his mentality, but I cannot diagnose it," he wrote. "It is not ordinary insanity, nor boyhood lack of understanding. He is untruthful and deceitful, cunning, and has no sense of responsibility. It suggests megalomania."

Anderson's parole was denied.

* * *

Frank W. Anderson served fifteen years in prison before being released in 1951. Anderson, then in his early 30s, continued his university education, finishing the few remaining courses he needed for a Bachelor of Arts then going on to a Masters in Social Work, which he completed in 1957.

But less than ten years after Anderson left prison he returned—this time as a parole officer, visiting inmates.

In the years that followed, Anderson worked with organizations like the John Howard Society and the Salvation Army as both an employee and volunteer. He developed and taught a social work program at Mount Royal College, and a scholarship was later formed there in his name. Prime Minister Pierre Trudeau pardoned Anderson in 1974 and appointed him to the National Parole Board. Anderson married, had children and grandchildren.

Throughout this life, Anderson passionately pursued his love of writing, penning and publishing a number of small history books, many about crime on the Prairies. He was known for his sense of humour and his compassion.

He died in Saskatoon on April 10, 2008 at the age of 88. An old man.

SOURCES AND REFERENCES

DEAD PARROTS—Court transcripts and documents; British Columbia court decisions; *Regina Leader-Post; Vancouver Sun; National Post; Vancouver Province;* interviews.

RED BLOOD IN THEIR VEINS—Court transcripts and documents; National Archives file; *Regina Morning Leader; Moose Jaw Evening Times.*

CYPRUS—Court transcripts; *Saskatoon StarPhoenix; Regina Leader-Post;* Canadian Press.

A FAITHFUL WIFE—Court transcripts, documents and exhibits; National Archives file; petition; *Regina Morning Leader.*

PAPER COWS—Court transcripts and documents; *Western Producer; Saskatoon StarPhoenix.*

TOOTSIE'S OATH—Court transcripts; National Archives file, *Regina Leader-Post, Sudbury Star.*

SOLDIER OF MISSED FORTUNE—Court transcripts; Saskatchewan Archives file; *Regina Morning Leader;* military records from National Archives; "Saskatchewan's Train Robbery" from *Outlaws of Saskatchewan* by Frank W. Anderson, Gopher Books; *Mahoney's Minute Men: The Saga of the Saskatchewan Provincial Police, 1917–1928* by Chris Stewart and Lynn Hudson, Modern Press,1978.

MORE THAN VIOLENCE—Court documents and transcripts; National Parole Board reports; reporter's notes and interviews; *Regina Leader-Post.*

RING AND RUN—Court transcripts and documents; *Regina Leader-Post;* reporter's notes.

THE PRISONER'S HEAD—Court transcripts; National Archives file; *Saskatoon Daily Phoenix;* "The Hungry Killer" from *Outlaws of Saskatchewan* by Frank W. Anderson, Gopher Books.

FROZEN ASSETS—Court transcripts and documents; *Regina Leader-Post.*

TIME BOMB—RCMP report; inquest report; *Regina Morning Leader; Regina Daily Post; Globe and Mail; Moose Jaw Murders and Other Deaths* by Bruce D. Fairman, Home Town Press, 2003.

BEGINNER'S LUCK—Court transcripts and documents; *Regina Leader-Post; Saskatoon StarPhoenix;* reporter's notes.

DEAR JOYCE—Court transcripts and documents, *Regina Leader-Post; Saskatoon StarPhoenix.*

TRAIN NUMBER SIX—Court transcripts; National Archives file; *Regina Leader-Post.*

TANGLED WEB—Court documents; reporter's notes; interviews.

THE SALESMEN—Court transcripts and documents; *Regina Leader-Post;* reporter's notes.

DORA AND THE DEVIL MAN—*Regina Leader-Post; Yorkton Enterprise; Melville Advance.*

THE SCHOOL MASTER—Court transcripts and documents; *Regina Leader-Post; Saskatoon StarPhoenix; Prince Albert Daily Herald.*

PUBLIC TRUST—Report of the Saskatchewan Canteen Funds Inquiry Commission, 1940; *Globe and Mail; Regina Leader-Post.*

HOSTAGE—"Gunman holds hostage, tells own story," by Al Rosseker, *Regina Leader-Post,* Feb. 9, 1973; other *Regina Leader-Post* articles; interviews.

A BITTER TASTE—Court transcript; Saskatchewan Archives file; *Regina Morning Leader;* Mack Sing v. Smith et al. (1908) 1 Saskatchewan Law Reports, 454.

LIPSTICK KISSES—Court transcripts and documents; *Saskatoon StarPhoenix;* Canadian Press.

JACK OF DIAMONDS—Court transcripts and documents; National Archives file, *Regina Morning Leader.*

LOOKING FOR MARY CATHERINE—Articles by Suzanne Boyer; *Moose Jaw Times Herald;* Blue Line Magazine; Internet postings by Shanahan's family; information from Moose Jaw Police Service.

FATHER AND SON—Court transcripts and documents; *Saskatoon StarPhoenix; Vancouver Sun;* Canwest News Service.

BAD BLOOD—Court transcripts; *Regina Leader-Post; Melville Advance.*

FEMALE AMBITION—Court transcripts and documents; *Regina Leader-Post.*

ALONE—Court transcripts and documents; National Archives file; *Regina Leader-Post.*

SEA OF FIRE—Court transcripts and documents; *Regina Leader-Post.*

TRAINS AND TROUBLE—Court transcripts and documents; court decisions from Ontario; *Regina Leader-Post; Moose Jaw Times Herald; Toronto Star;* Canadian Press; *Globe and Mail; Moose Jaw Murders and Other Deaths* by Bruce D. Fairman, Home Town Press, 2003.

THE ETHICS OF PURCHASING—Court transcripts and documents; *Saskatoon StarPhoenix;* "Thief excelled at fiction" by Matthew Coutts, *National Post; Library Journal;* "The Ethics of Purchasing—The Wheatland Position" by Bruce Cameron.

LADIES' MAN—Court transcripts and documents; reporter's notes and interviews; Canadian Press; Saskatchewan News Network; *Regina Leader-Post.*

UNCLE GEORGE—Court transcripts; National Archives file; *Regina Morning Leader; Winnipeg Free Press;* "The Killer and The Kids" from *Outlaws of Saskatchewan* by Frank W. Anderson, Gopher Books.

MANHUNT—*Saskatoon Star-Phoenix; Regina Leader-Post.*

THE FOREST RANGER—Court transcripts and documents; *Regina Morning Leader.*

MIDDLE-AGED CROOKS—Court transcripts and documents; *Regina Leader-Post.*

THE KILLING ROOM—Court documents and transcripts; *Regina Leader-Post.*

STRONGER THAN DEATH—Court documents, transcripts and videotapes; *Regina Leader-Post;* reporter's notes and interviews.

A MODEL PRISONER—Poetry excerpt from "Some Experiments in Rhythm" by Frank W. Anderson, 1942 as contained in National Archives file; court transcripts and documents; biographical information from BC Author Bank, Gopher Books and Frank Anderson's obituary notice; *Regina Leader-Post.*

ABOUT THE AUTHORS

Jana G. Pruden (left) is a graduate of the Nova Scotia College of Art and Design, and has a Bachelor of Fine Arts. She's been reporting on court and crime for the *Regina-Leader Post* since 2003, and is also a columnist.

Born and raised in Regina, Barb Pacholik (right) is a graduate of the University of Regina's School of Journalism. Since 1988 she has worked as a reporter at the *Regina-Leader Post*, where most of her career has been spent covering crime and justice issues.

This is their second collection of true Saskatchewan crime stories.

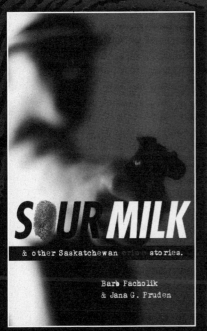